Literary CAMBRIDGE

Literary CAMBRIDGE

LISA SARGOOD

SUTTON PUBLISHING

Sutton Publishing Limited
Phoenix Mill · Thrupp · Stroud
Gloucestershire · GL5 2BU

First published 2004

Half-title page photograph: Pembroke Library.
(*Cambridgeshire Collection, Cambridge Central Library*)
Title page photograph: Students picnicking in
The Orchard, Grantchester. (*Cambridgeshire Collection, Cambridge Central Library*)

British Library Cataloguing in Publication Data
A catalogue record for this book is available from the British Library.

ISBN 0-7509-2288-5

Typeset in 10.5/13.5 Photina.
Typesetting and origination by
Sutton Publishing Limited.
Printed and bound in England by
J.H. Haynes & Co. Ltd, Sparkford.

This book is dedicated with love to my father,
L.J. Sargood (1921–2003).

CONTENTS

King's gateway and view of college, showing rooftops of Queens' College. *(S. Roberts Collection)*

Cambridge is a delight of a place, now there is nobody in it.
Thomas Gray

A city like any other . . . were it not for the order at the centre and the high,
invisible bridge it is built upon.
Ann Stevenson

An asylum – in more senses than one.
A.E. Housman

. . . nor is there want of mirth and good company of other kinds.
Daniel Defoe

Cambridge, the mother of Poets . . .
Leslie Stephen

Cambridge is the only place I never want to leave, though I suffer more there than
anywhere else.
Lytton Strachey

INTRODUCTION

Embarking on a book entitled *Literary Cambridge* is a foolhardy endeavour. The city has played host to such a wealth of creative talent across the centuries that it is hard to know where to begin the tale and even more difficult to know where to finish. Equally taxing is who to include and who to leave out, while at every turn you meet an expert upon the life and work of your subjects.

Both city and university are riddled with the tales of poets, playwrights, novelists, satirists, diarists, biographers, scriptwriters and others. Each short caption in this book seeks to give a rare glimpse of character and story and each picture to reveal a lost aspect of the place, as captured by the photographers and painters who loved Cambridge – a unique world which has inspired some of the greatest minds in history.

Wordsworth, Tennyson and Byron loved the poetic atmosphere fostered by their predecessors, the romantic imagination being quick to feel a sense of connection with centuries of literary sensibility in a place. Both Wordsworth and Tennyson wrote poems upon visiting Milton's mulberry tree at Christ's. They would not have denied that the friendships they forged and the artistic, spiritual and academic influences they were exposed to in Cambridge fed the direction of their lives and works. Love it or hate it, the experience of Cambridge can prove formative.

Clive James remembers: 'In Cambridge, I began to find my way. . . . In Cambridge I could develop all my propensities, such as they were, to the fullest extent possible, and all at once. The result was chaos.' (*May Week was in June*)

Cambridge minds offer a remarkable diversity of literary talent and works featuring the city abound. Through such writing the Cambridge influence extends beyond its geography and becomes truly international. Generations of students have argued the merits of Byron over Shelley, Coleridge above Wordsworth, and reviewed Shakespeare from wide-ranging perspectives, many first thought through in the rooms of a Cambridge college.

The novelist A.S. Byatt recalls: 'I used to have a conversation from time to time with Iris Murdoch about whether there were such things as the "Cambridge mind" and the "Oxford mind". I came to the conclusion . . . that I do have a Cambridge mind – empirical, pragmatic, puritanical, reasonable, sympathetic towards science – as opposed to an Oxford romanticism. . . .'

Cambridge never fails to stimulate, inspire and affect those whose paths take them through the city, and now Cambridge is less detached from London the hothouse atmosphere is not so much diffused as infused. Yet the impact of the local environment has remained strong. It appears and reappears in novel after novel, century after century: as the backdrop to P.D. James's detective fiction, E.M. Forster's most

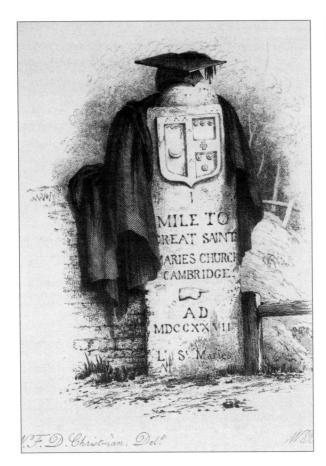

Milestone with gown and mortar board. *(Cambridgeshire Collection, Cambridge Central Library)*

evocative novels and many others. Those who wish to read more will find a selection of books by and about the city, university and student life at the end of this work.

I have been fortunate to receive the help of a number of contemporary authors, whose comments upon the influence of the city and university on their lives and work have been enlightening. I am grateful to A.S. Byatt, Clive James, Colin Dexter, J.G. Ballard, Margaret Drabble, P.D. James, Dr Mary Archer and others for permission to reproduce their photographs and writings in this book. The Masters and Fellows of many colleges were also very supportive and many of their alumni feature here. My thanks are due to them for permission to reproduce college portraits and statues.

With a literary history this rich to explore the visitor could spend a year in Cambridge absorbing the atmosphere. This book is intended as a guide for those with a week or a weekend in the city. I hope that the decisions I have made offer the reader, whether knowledgeable about literary history or simply intrigued, enough detail to bring to life some of the stories that abound and a few surprises from its more unlikely corners.

For those seeking greater depth I highly recommend Graham Chainey's book *A Literary History of Cambridge*, and Charles Moseley and Clive Wilmer's *Cambridge Observed, An Anthology*.

Lisa Sargood, 2004

1

Cambridge, Town & Gown

Members of the Bull Book Club, established in 1784.
(Cambridgeshire Collection, Cambridge Central Library)

Above: The elegant and imposing Fitzwilliam Museum in Trumpington Street was built between 1837 and 1847 to house the bequests of the wealthy collector Viscount Fitzwilliam. The collection includes illustrations by Blake, including *The Tyger*, and has a life mask of the poet. It also possesses portraits of Thomas Hardy and George Bernard Shaw and the court suit of Samuel Rogers, worn subsequently by both Wordsworth and Tennyson at their installations as Poet Laureate. *(Cambridgeshire Collection, Cambridge Central Library)*

The entrance hall to the Fitzwilliam Museum. Manuscripts owned by the museum include Keats's *Ode to a Nightingale*, Rupert Brooke's *The Old Vicarage, Grantchester*, A.E. Housman's *Last Poems* and Thomas Hardy's *Jude the Obscure*. *(Reproduced by permission of the Fitzwilliam Museum, Cambridge)*

William Blake (1757–1827), poet, engraver and mystic, has been a profound influence on other artists and writers through the centuries. Although Blake was never a resident of Cambridge, the Fitzwilliam Museum is home to a number of his most famous works, including the poem *The Tyger* and his life mask. *(Reproduced by permission of the Fitzwilliam Museum, Cambridge)*

The Fitzwilliam Museum also possesses Blake's beautiful *The Ancient of Days*. Blake was an important influence on Rupert Brooke. On 3 August 1908 Geoffrey Keynes gave the young poet a collection of Blake's verse which was to affect Brooke's poetry considerably, taking his work off in a new mystical direction. *(Reproduced by permission of the Fitzwilliam Museum, Cambridge)*

The original manuscripts by John Keats (1795–1821) for 'Ode to a Nightingale' are also in the possession of the Fitzwilliam Museum. (*Reproduced by permission of the Fitzwilliam Museum, Cambridge*)

The Eagle pub. Elizabethan England had a rich dramatic life, despite bans on wandering players and theatrical companies. The Lord Chamberlain's Company was a group of professional strolling actors which, at this time, counted William Shakespeare among its number. They visited Cambridge in 1595 and possibly again in 1602. Their first performance is thought to have been *Hamlet* (legend tells that Shakespeare took the role of the Ghost). It was common for players to perform in venues like the Eagle, where the gallery allows for a tiered audience or can be used for balcony scenes, as in *Romeo and Juliet*.

Charles Dickens (1812–70) was a very popular visitor to Cambridge, and came to the city on three occasions while travelling the country on public reading tours. In October 1859 he stayed at the Eagle while appearing at the Guildhall to read from *Dombey and Son*. In March 1867 he returned and read from *Pickwick Papers*. For his last appearance, in March 1869, Dickens gave 'One Farewell Reading' to an avid audience of academics and townspeople.

A century later, Clive James commented, 'The Eagle was the most romantic pub in Cambridge, if not the whole of England. During the war, bomber crews from all over East Anglia had come to the Eagle to spend, in hilarious conviviality, what was statistically likely to be one of their last evenings alive.' (*May Week Was In June*) (*Cambridgeshire Collection, Cambridge Central Library*)

Falcon Yard, now demolished. The taverns and inns of Cambridge can be viewed as the alternative Alma Mater of the city's literary talent. In February 1660, while visiting his father and brother John (who was about to be admitted to Christ's), Samuel Pepys stayed at the Falcon Inn in Falcon Yard, Petty Cury, near the market square. This inn is conjectured as another venue for performances by companies of Elizabethan players and so may also have played host to Shakespeare. One of Pepys's favourite meeting places was the Rose (now demolished, it was in Rose Crescent) and he also frequented the Three Tuns (formerly at the corner of Market Hill and St Edward's Passage). *(Cambridgeshire Collection, Cambridge Central Library)*

Tritinty Street, *c.* 1910. In about 1629 Thomas Randolph (1605–35), noted Cambridge wit, poet, playwright and later friend of the dramatist Ben Jonson, penned a wonderful satire on one of the frequent Town/Gown disputes, *The Townsmen's Petition of Cambridge*, which remarks that if the King intervenes, the people will have no choice but to retract their objections:

> The Townsmen they must hang
> the head,
> And Scholars must domineer.

(Cambridgeshire Collection, Cambridge Central Library)

The Bell. Randolph left Cambridge in 1630 when plague forced closure of the University, but returned in 1631 (after time in London where he wrote plays for the King's Revels) to take his MA. His plays, including *The Conceited Peddler* and *Hey for Honesty*, feature many references to Cambridge inns, particularly the Rose and Mitre, their landlords being lauded as the 'best tutors in the universities'. *(Cambridgeshire Collection, Cambridge Central Library)*

Above: Near the corner of Rose Crescent and Market Hill, portrayed here in the late eighteenth century, was the site of Bacon's tobacconist's shop, which was frequented by many of Cambridge's undergraduate literary types, including Tennyson, despite a ban on smoking by the University. Tennyson was a heavy pipe smoker from the age of 14. (*Reproduced by permission of the Fitzwilliam Museum, Cambridge*)

C.S. Calverley was elected a Fellow of Christ's College in 1858. In 1862 he wrote of his passion for smoking in 'Ode to Tobacco', which can still be seen written on a brass plaque on the wall of what was Bacon's tobacco shop. One of his contemporaries was W.W. Skeat, Professor of Anglo-Saxon (1878–1912), and the editor of *Piers Plowman* and *The Complete Works of Chaucer* (1894–7). (*Author*)

Above: King's Parade, *c.* 1920s. At 11 King's Parade a plaque commemorates the visit of Charles and Mary Lamb, who were both very fond of Cambridge. Another at no. 19 indicates the residence of Edward Fitzgerald (Trinity undergraduate 1827–30, author of *Euphranor* and, most famously, translator of *The Rubaiyat of Omar Khayyam*) during his Cambridge years. Tennyson also stayed in rooms along the parade.

Mary and Charles Lamb frequently walked The Backs (the tree-lined path along the river behind the colleges) with Crabb Robinson, who wrote in his diary that they spent the whole visit walking 'out of one college into another'. In 1820 Charles Lamb wrote *Oxford in the Vacation*, his recollections of time at Oxford and Cambridge Universities. (*Cambridgeshire Collection, Cambridge Central Library*)

Left: Lord Byron was fated to lose several of his closest friends in tragic circumstances. Within the walls of St Benet's Church, near Corpus Christi College, is a plaque to the memory of his confidant Charles Matthews, who drowned in the Cam after becoming entangled in weeds. Byron was heartbroken. (*Author*)

A portrait of Henry and William James, taken in 1900 by Marie Leon. The American novelist Henry James (1843–1916), author of *The Bostonians* (1886), *The Wings of the Dove* (1902) and many other novels, visited Cambridge on several occasions. He is known to have stayed at 8 Trumpington Street and Leckhampton House (now part of Corpus Christi College).

In *English Vignettes* (1879) James describes a beautiful morning in Cambridge, with 'the loveliest confusion of Gothic windows and ancient trees', where 'the thin-flowing Cam appears to exist simply as an occasion for these brave little bridges – the beautiful covered gallery of John's or the slightly-collapsing arch of Clare'.

James revisited Cambridge in July 1884 and lunched with F.W.H. Myers at Leckhampton House, off Grange Road. Myers was a great friend of George Eliot and she visited him here often.

He returned in June 1909, during which visit he breakfasted with John Maynard Keynes, lunched with Geoffrey Keynes and met Rupert Brooke. James asked if Brooke was a 'good poet' and, on being told that he wasn't, replied, 'Thank goodness. If he looked like that and was a good poet too, I do not know what I should do.' Upon hearing of Brooke's death James commented sadly on 'the wasted grace of such a person'. (*National Portrait Gallery*)

A tram at the corner of Regent Street, *c.* 1910. The Cambridge University Fabian Society was founded in 1906 and invited both H.G. Wells and George Bernard Shaw to speak there. It was here that Wells first met Rupert Brooke. Wells advocated radical reform of the university system to allow greater access by the ordinary man and woman.

Wells put his visits to the city to literary use. In his book *The New Machiavelli* (1911) Wells's hero studies at Trinity College and says, 'Cambridge is a world of subdued tones, of excessively subtle humours, of prim conduct and free thinking.' *(Cambridgeshire Collection, Cambridge Central Library)*

A bridge on the Backs, *c.* 1900. The American poet Ezra Pound came to Cambridge in 1912 to visit his friend T.E. Hulme (1883–1917), poet and argumentative Modernist, who lodged in the city. *(Cambridgeshire Collection, Cambridge Central Library)*

A mid-nineteenth-century view of Grantchester Street. Sir Walter Scott (1771–1832) has two associations with Cambridge. He used the story of the Knight Gervase in his tale connected with Wandlebury (an outlying ancient village) and Scott also received £100 for reviewing the decoded versions of Pepys's diaries. *(Cambridgeshire Collection, Cambridge Central Library)*

In December 1925, T.E. Lawrence (1888–1935), better known as 'Lawrence of Arabia' and author of *Seven Pillars of Wisdom*, visited Cambridge to see E.M. Forster at the 'splendiferous' King's. In February 1935, when his brother A.W. Lawrence was living at 31 Madingley Road (shown here), Lawrence returned to Cambridge, having cycled from Brighton after leaving the RAF. Just three months later he was killed in a motorcycle accident in Dorset. *(Author)*

Mill Road, *c.* 1930. Dylan Thomas stayed at 274a Mill Road in March 1937, while visiting Cambridge to give a reading at St John's College. Apparently, so the story goes, they held a week-long drinking party at which the poet was guest of honour. (*Cambridgeshire Collection, Cambridge Central Library*)

The academic career of the most famous British detective has long been the subject of debate. The crime writer Dorothy L. Sayers claimed that Sherlock Holmes was a student of chemistry at Sidney Sussex College, though others have suggested Peterhouse and Trinity. Tantalisingly, legend tells that there was a student by the name of Moriarty enrolled at Trinity College in the late nineteenth century. Holmes visits Cambridge in a number of Conan Doyle's stories including *The Missing Three-Quarter*. (*Cambridgeshire Collection, Cambridge Central Library*)

In 1843 17 Trinity Street housed the premises of Daniel and Alexander Macmillan, booksellers. Later they moved to no. 1, at the corner near Great St Mary's Church (now Cambridge University Press – the site had been a bookseller's since 1581). Macmillan were the publishers of Charles Kingsley and their shop was a meeting place for all manner of literary figures. It was at no. 17 that Tennyson gave the first public reading of his poem *Maud*. (*Cambridgeshire Collection, Cambridge Central Library*)

Heffers bookshop at the corner of Sidney Street and Market Square, *c.* 1950. Through the centuries bookshops have become almost as much a feature of Cambridge as the colleges. It would be easy to spend several days browsing in them all. (*Cambridgeshire Collection, Cambridge Central Library*)

University Library from Great St Mary's. *(S. Roberts Collection)*

Cambridge University Library is a copyright library, housing at least one copy of every book published in the UK. It holds one of the most fascinating collections of literary manuscripts in the world. Among the rarities in the Manuscripts Room are the letters and poems (several illustrated by the poet) of Siegfried Sassoon, a graduate of Clare College. In 1992 the Library bought back a collection of poems presented by the University of Cambridge to Queen Elizabeth I in 1564.

It also possesses a number of special collections, including musical manuscripts, rare Bibles and other rare or unique papers and letters. Access is possible by appointment. Apply to the University Library (www.lib.cam.ac.uk).

> Stephanie remembered other libraries, still wool-gathering. Principally the Cambridge University Library in the summer of her finals. She remembered the sensation of knowledge, of grasping an argument, seizing an illustration, seeing a link, a connection, between this ancient Greek idea here and this seventeenth-century English one, in other words.
>
> A.S. Byatt, *The Virgin in the Garden.*

2

The Royal Colleges –
Trinity, King's & St John's

A statue of Henry VIII in the gateway of Trinity College.
(Cambridgeshire Collection, Cambridge Central Library)

Trinity College was founded in 1546 by King Henry VIII and created by bringing together three smaller Halls. It is now the largest and richest of the Cambridge colleges, with an impressive list of literary alumni.

In the sixteenth century these included poet and dramatist George Gascoigne, Dr John Dee (thought to have been Shakespeare's inspiration for Prospero in *The Tempest*), diarist Francis Bacon and poet Giles Fletcher the Younger (1588–1623). Fletcher was just one of a whole family of alumni, which included the dramatist John Fletcher (1579–1625). John came up to Corpus Christi College and went on to write, with his collaborator Beaumont, a number of highly successful Jacobean comedies.

During the seventeenth century the college was attended by a number of poets and dramatists, including George Herbert, John Suckling, Abraham Cowley, Andrew Marvell, Poet Laureate John Dryden and Nathaniel Lee. Abraham Cowley lived at Trinity College until 1644 when he was removed from his Fellowship by the Parliamentarians.

Trinity's eighteenth-century poets included George Crabbe and Lord Byron. Laurence Eusden, Fellow of Trinity College and Poet Laureate after 1717, was subjected to Alexander Pope's satirical pen, appearing as a character in *The Dunciad* (1728).

In the nineteenth century the novelists Edward Bulwer-Lytton and William Makepeace Thackeray and the poets Alfred Lord Tennyson, Edward Fitzgerald, Edmund Gosse and A.E. Housman went to Trinity College. Thackeray (1811–63) and T.B. Macaulay (Fellow 1824) both had rooms on Trinity's E staircase, as did the hero of Thackeray's novel *The History of Henry Esmond* (1852).

Twentieth-century alumni include biographer Lytton Strachey, editor and publisher Leonard Woolf, literary critic Clive Bell, authors A.A. Milne, Vladimir Nabokov and Nicholas Monsarrat, critic and novelist Raymond Williams, and playwrights Peter Schaffer and Simon Gray. (*Cambridgeshire Collection, Cambridge Central Library*)

The Great Hall, Trinity College. Built in 1608, the hall at Trinity College was more than an eating place. It was designed as a fully functioning theatre and constructed to outdo St John's hall, which had become a magnet for actors and lecturers. The stage, seating and galleries were elaborate, being cut from oak timbers and marked for swift assembly whenever a play was to be performed.

This dramatic tradition continues. Trinity College can count among its alumni a remarkable number of playwrights, directors and producers, including more recently Stephen Frears (Trinity 1960), director of *My Beautiful Laundrette*, *Prick Up Your Ears*, *Dangerous Liaisons*, *High Fidelity* and *The Snapper*. *(Cambridgeshire Collection, Cambridge Central Library)*

Great Court, Trinity College. At one time the fountain here was the source of the college's drinking water.

In Tudor England, while professional players may have been discouraged, student productions were positively encouraged. Plays are recorded at Queens' College, Trinity College and St John's College at this time. The first play performed at Trinity College was John Dee's *Peace* in 1546. Dr Dee , Court Astrologer to Elizabeth I, possessed England's finest library, a huge collection of Latin, Greek and alchemical texts, much of which was destroyed when a mob ransacked his home in Mortlake.

Robert Louis Stevenson (1850–94) came to Cambridge in October 1878 and stayed in Great Court, A staircase. He found the college atmosphere unconducive to writing.

Henry James felt differently: 'What institution is more majestic than Trinity College? The first quadrangle is of immense extent, and the buildings that surround it, with their long, rich fronts of time-deepened gray, are the stateliest in the world.'

Lytton Strachey (Trinity 1899–1903) lived in rooms on K staircase. Here he formed friendships with Leonard Woolf, Clive Bell and Thoby Stephen, so founding the collective later known as the Bloomsbury Group. Strachey won the Chancellor's Medal for poetry but is better known for *Eminent Victorians* (1918). *(Author)*

John Dryden (1631–1700), the first Poet Laureate, was born at Aldwinkle, Northamptonshire, and educated at Westminster School and Trinity College, Cambridge. He excelled in Classics. His first major work was *Heroic Stanzas* (1658), written to commemorate Cromwell's death. This was closely followed by poems in praise of the restoration of the monarchy. His political satire *Absalom and Achitophel* appeared in 1681. Although he was a controversial figure during his lifetime (he lost the Laureateship in 1688), his literary status assured him burial in Westminster Abbey. *(Reproduced by permission of The Master & Fellows of Trinity College, Cambridge)*

The poet Andrew Marvell (1621–78) was a Trinity undergraduate and contributor to *Musa Cantabrigensis*. He remained in residence at Cambridge for several years, but had a somewhat contentious relationship with the university. After converting to Catholicism he left for London but his father pursued him and convinced him to resume his studies. Marvell eventually left the city in 1640 after his father's death.

A committed republican, he lived through and commented upon England's most critical political years, penning 'An Horatian Ode upon Cromwell's Return from Ireland' (1650) and an elegy on Cromwell's death.

Marvell was a friend of John Milton. Although he is now well known for his poems, very few were published during his lifetime. Three years after his death *Miscellaneous Poems* was printed; this included 'To His Coy Mistress', one of his best-known poems. *Poems on Affairs of State* was published in 1689. *(Reproduced by permission of The Master & Fellows of Trinity College, Cambridge)*

The elegant Wren Library has the manuscripts of Milton's epic *Comus*, Thackeray's *Henry Esmond*, A.A. Milne's *Winnie-the-Pooh* and some of Byron's letters. There is also a Tennyson archive and Thorwaldsen's statue of Lord Byron, which was refused by Westminster Abbey. Celia Fiennes praised Grinling Gibbons's work in the library as 'the finest carving of wood in flowers, birds, leaves . . . as ever I saw'. (Not open to the public.) *(Author)*

Alan Alexander Milne (1882–1956) entered Trinity College in 1900 from Westminster School. He contributed short pieces to *Granta* during his time at the university and later became its editor. He is best known as the author of *Winnie-the-Pooh*. (*Photograph by Howard Coster, 1926, National Portrait Gallery*)

Winnie-the-Pooh goes visiting.

After completing his degree Milne gained a position on the humorous magazine *Punch*, but he is of course most famous for his endearing creation *Winnie-the-Pooh*. This extract is from part of a manuscript held in the Wren Library. (*Reproduced by permission of the Master and Fellows of Trinity College, Cambridge*)

D.H. Lawrence (1885–1930), author of *Sons and Lovers* (1913) and *The Rainbow* (1915), visited Cambridge in March 1915 at the invitation of Bertrand Russell. It was during the First World War and both were conscientious objectors. Lawrence was evidently a little awed by the prospect and wrote to his friend, 'I feel frightfully important coming to Cambridge – quite momentous the occasion is for me.' He had recently completed *The Rainbow* and was looking forward to the diversion. While there he dined with John Maynard Keynes in Russell's rooms in Neville's Court (the Cloisters were at that time a military hospital), an experience which unsettled him. He left shortly afterwards and later wrote to Russell that 'Cambridge made me very black and down. I cannot bear its smell of rottenness. . . .' (*Author*)

This statue of Sir Francis Bacon (1561–1626) can be seen in Trinity College chapel. This influential Elizabethan thinker, statesman and essayist heavily criticised the outmoded Aristotelian teaching system propounded at Cambridge in his work *The Advancement of Learning*. He arrived in Cambridge in 1573 with his brother Anthony but left three years later, transferring to Gray's Inn. He was later to represent Cambridge in parliament. His collection of writings, *Essays*, was published in 1597. (*Reproduced by permission of the Master and Fellows of Trinity College, Cambridge*)

A.E. Housman (1859–1936), Professor of Latin (1911) and Fellow of Trinity, was the author of the acclaimed *A Shropshire Lad* (1896), *Last Poems* (1922) and *More Poems* (1936). (*Drawing by Rothenstein, reproduced by permission of the Masters and Fellows of Trinity College, Cambridge*)

A.E. Housman memorial plaque in Trinity College chapel. Along the Backs at Trinity is an avenue of cherry trees that was planted in memory of Housman. (*Cambridgeshire Collection, Cambridge Central Library*)

The statue of Alfred, 1st Baron Tennyson (1809–92) in Trinity Chapel. The chapel also houses statues of Macaulay and Bacon as well as beautiful brass memorial plaques to a number of other literary men. (*Author*)

Rose Crescent. Tennyson (1809–92) arrived in Cambridge on 9 November 1827, and lodged for a time with his brothers Frederick and Charles at 12 Rose Crescent, where he kept a pet snake in his room. (*Cambridgeshire Collection, Cambridge Central Library*)

The portrait of Tennyson in Trinity College. The Tennyson brothers were all admitted to study at Trinity College. In April 1828 they moved to rooms at 57 Corpus Buildings, Trumpington Street, where Alfred remained until he left Cambridge. Tennyson won the Chancellor's Medal in 1829 with his poem 'Timbuctoo'. It was at Trinity that he met and befriended Arthur Hallam (1811–33), who had rooms at G3 New Court, Trinity. It was this friendship and Hallam's untimely death that inspired some of Tennyson's finest poetry, including 'In Memoriam'. Tennyson became member no. 70 of the Society of Apostles (formerly the Cambridge Conversazione Society, founded at St John's College in 1820) in October 1829. He was very affected by the literary history of the city and made 'pilgrimages', including to Christ's College to find Milton's Mulberry tree and to Grantchester to swim at Byron's Pool (which according to legend was the inspiration behind his poem 'The Lady of Shallot'). He was, however, highly dismissive of his tutors, writing in 'Lines on Cambridge' (1830):

> . . . you that do profess to teach,
> And teach us nothing, feeding not the heart.

Perhaps Trinity's most famous student was Lord Byron (George Gordon, 6th Baron Byron, 1788–1824). *(Reproduced by permission of The Master & Fellows of Trinity College, Cambridge)*

The infamous Lord Byron followed his forebears to Trinity College in October 1805, though he would have preferred to go to Oxford with his friends from Harrow. The boy who later became the charismatic poet was then shy, fat and had a club foot. After a few weeks, however, he wrote to his sister, 'I like College Life extremely . . . I am now most pleasantly situated in *Super*excellent Rooms . . . I am allowed 500 a year, a Servant and Horse, so Feel as independent as a German Prince.'

The location of Byron's rooms has long been the subject of debate. Tradition holds that they were on K Staircase of Great Court, although I1 on Nevile's Court (first floor, middle north side) is another possible location.

In common with many other students of literary sensibility Byron was taken aback by apparent lack of scholarship. He noted that 'nobody here seems to look into an author ancient or modern if they can avoid it'.

In 1843 a full-length statue of the poet by Thorwaldsen, originally intended for Westminster Abbey, was brought to Cambridge and housed in Trinity College Library.

As a Lord, Byron held certain privileges which included dining with the dons at High Table and the opportunity to wear a highly ornate gown. He was a spectacle in the city streets, not least because of his habit of wearing a tall white hat instead of a black one.

Byron spent lavishly while at Cambridge (and after visits to London he often reappeared stylishly in a carriage and four), much to the chagrin of his lawyer, Hanson.

Byron left Cambridge for a time and escaped into the country where he wrote *Fugitive Pieces*, later called *Poems on Various Occasions* and *Hours of Idleness*. He also wrote two satires about Cambridge, 'Granta: A Medley' and 'Thoughts Suggested by a College Examination'. In 'Granta: A Medley' he wrote:

> There, in apartments small and damp,
> The candidate for college prizes
> Sits poring by the midnight lamp;
> Goes late to bed, yet early rises . . .

His poetry won little applause from the tutors and when asked to explain his absences he replied that Cambridge had nothing to teach him. His early love affair with the university was evidently over: 'I have other Reasons for not residing at Cambridge, I dislike it; I . . . can never consider Granta as my "Alma Mater" but rather as a Nurse of no very promising appearance.'

Typically, however, he altered his plans to leave and stayed another year, forming friendships with John Cam Hobhouse (1786–1869) and Scrope Berdmore Davies (1783–1852). When Davies's bank vault was opened (in 1976) it was found to contain manuscripts attributed to Byron and Shelley. Byron left Cambridge for good in December 1807.

Trinity Master's Lodge, Byron's bear tower. The myth still persists that Byron kept a live bear in Trinity Great Court, near the present Master's Lodge. The home of his tame bear is said to have been in a hexagonal room in this tower. A bill sent to Byron for 'stabling' indicates, however, that it was actually kept at Ram Yard near the Round Church. Keeping a live bear as a pet was not an unusual aristocratic pastime. Byron eventually sent his bear home to Newstead Abbey. (*Author*)

Byron and his friends Edward Long and John Edleston spent long hours swimming at what is now called 'Byron's Pool', a millpond upstream from Grantchester. He wrote of it, 'Though Cam's is not a very "translucent wave", it was fourteen feet deep, where we used to dive for . . . plates, eggs, and even shillings'. (*Cambridgeshire Collection, Cambridge Central Library*)

The author André Gide stayed at the so-called Byron's Lodge in Grantchester in 1918. No one is quite sure how it acquired this association. Gide then moved into Cambridge, staying at Merton House, Queens Road. (*Cambridgeshire Collection, Cambridge Central Library*)

Above: Nabokov's rooms in Trinity Lane. Vladimir Nabokov (1899–1977; Trinity 1919–23) said in *Speak, Memory* (1951) that while a student at Cambridge he never once went to the University Library or to lectures but spent most of his time in London. He described his rooms in Trinity Lane as 'intolerably squalid' yet his recollections of the city are highly nostalgic. While an undergraduate he translated *Alice in Wonderland* and the poems of Rupert Brooke, among other works, into Russian. His novel *Glory* is mostly set in Cambridge. (*Author*)

Whelwell's Court – the rooms of Thom Gunn. The poet Thom Gunn (1929–2004; Trinity 1950) was a student at Trinity College reading English. After graduating he moved to America to teach at Berkeley. He was quoted as saying, 'As an undergraduate I was enormously happy at Cambridge but now when I return there I do get a strong feeling of claustrophobia.' He began writing poetry in earnest while a student here and by his second year was well known as a Cambridge poet, with reviews of his work appearing in *Granta*. (*Author*)

Situated in the heart of Cambridge, bridging Market Hill and the Backs, King's College possesses some of the most beautiful and imposing medieval buildings in the city, photographed here in about 1900. The foundation stone of the 'College roial of Oure Lady and Seynt Nicholas' was laid by Henry VI on Passion Sunday 1441. The institution housed 70 scholars taken directly from Eton (a tradition which lasted for 400 years).

King's literary alumni include the poet Rupert Brooke, poet and ambassador Giles Fletcher (*c.* 1549–1611), Sir John Harington, friend of Shakespeare (1561–1612), novelist and letter-writer Sir Horace Walpole (1717–97), poet and peace-worker G. Lowes Dickinson (1862–1932), ghost story writer M.R. James (1862–1936), author E.M. Forster (1879–1970), novelist and Nobel Laureate Patrick White (1912–90) and Salman Rushdie (graduated 1965), author of *The Satanic Verses* and *Midnight's Children*. (*Cambridgeshire Collection, Cambridge Central Library*)

King's gateway and Chapel, mid-eighteenth century. The Chapel dominates the skyline and the gatehouse is an elaborate monument to Victorian eccentricity. The elegant Regency-period Fellows' Building was the home of E.M. Forster. John Betjeman, former Poet Laureate, wrote a poem about King's College published in 1954, and called it 'the most Oxford-like' of Cambridge colleges. (*Cambridgeshire Collection, Cambridge Central Library*)

A side view of King's Chapel. (*S. Roberts Collection*)

In The Prelude (III, lines 1–17) Wordsworth wrote:

> . . . nothing cheered our way till first we saw
> The long-roofed chapel of King's College lift . . .

He rapturously described the Chapel in a sonnet from about 1820:

> . . . that branching roof
> Self-poised, and scooped into ten thousand cells,
> Where light and shade repose, where music dwells
> Lingering – and wandering on as loth to die . . .

King's College Chapel. The war memorial in the chapel lists Rupert Brooke's name. *(Cambridgeshire Collection, Cambridge Central Library)*

She walked gravely down the length of Trinity Library, visited the Old Schools, sat quietly at the back of King's College Chapel marvelling at the upward surge of John Wastell's great vault spreading into curved fans of delicate white stone. The sunlight pouring through the great windows staining the still air, blue, crimson and green. The finely carved Tudor roses, the heraldic beasts supporting the crown, stood out in arrogant pride from the panels. Despite what Milton and Wordsworth had written, surely this chapel had been built to the glory of an earthly sovereign, not to the service of God?

P.D. James, *An Unsuitable Job for a Woman*

Below: A view of the chapel from Queens'. Wordsworth's attachment to this grand building was felt by Thomas Hardy, who during a walk there one late evening in October 1880 believed he sensed the poet's ghost wandering there. Hardy also climbed the chapel roof to take in the extent of the city. *(Cambridgeshire Collection, Cambridge Central Library)*

King's College Founder's Building and the west end of the chapel. Oscar Wilde (1854–1900) was a devoted Oxford man but visited Cambridge on at least two occasions. His close friend Robert Ross was at King's College and in November of 1879 Wilde was a guest of Oscar Browning there. While in the city Wilde attended a performance at the ADC Theatre and met the cast. In November 1885 he returned as guest of The Cicadas, a literary group. He is said to have contrived *The Happy Prince* during this visit. Wilde's son Vyvyan Holland (1886–1967) discreetly entered Trinity Hall in 1905 to read law. (*Cambridgeshire Collection, Cambridge Central Library*)

Rupert Brooke had rooms in the Fellows' Building in 1906. He was elected an Apostle – a member of an elite debating society only open to members of Trinity and King's Colleges. He also joined the Fabians and began to contribute poems and reviews to the *Cambridge Review*, and was a founder member of the Marlowe Society, which still performs today.

In 1909 Rupert left King's for quieter rooms at The Orchard in Grantchester. He moved shortly after into the Old Vicarage, Grantchester, the subject of one of his most famous poems. Here he also wrote a thesis on Webster which, at second submission, won him a King's Fellowship. (*Photograph by Sherril Schell 1913, reproduced by permission of the Rupert Brooke Society and the Provost & Fellows of King's College, Cambridge*)

E.M. Forster (1879–1970), author of *Howard's End* and *A Room with A View*, both memorably filmed by Merchant Ivory, read Classics and History at King's between 1897 and 1901 and, like Rupert Brooke, was elected to the Society of Apostles. He became a Fellow in 1927. In 1946 he took rooms on A staircase and remained there until his death. *The Longest Journey*, published in 1907, is set partly in Cambridge and describes the city and university with a heart-felt affection. The narrator tells of how Cambridge had soothed him, 'warmed him and had laughed at him a little, saying that he must not be so tragic . . .'. (*Drawing by Edmond Kapp 1930, reproduced by permission of the Provost & Fellows of King's College, Cambridge*)

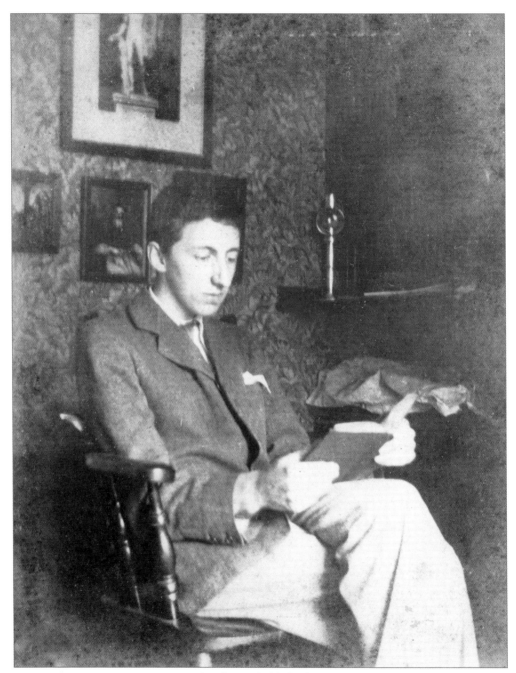

E.M. Forster as a young man. King's Library holds both Forster's archives and also those of Rupert Brooke, and has a growing collection of modern literary manuscripts, including the papers of Rosamond Lehmann and Louis MacNeice. (*Reproduced by permission of the Provost & Fellows of King's College, Cambridge*)

In her novel *The Virgin in the Garden* A.S. Byatt provides a pen portrait of E.M. Forster when he was somewhat older:

> The tea party was in rooms overlooking the main court, across to the chapel. The novelist sat, small, old, secret, benign, moustached, in a chintz-covered armchair. . . . The novelist spoke of punting, of how time had seemed slower in his Cambridge.

Tea on the lawn, *c.* 1918. Forster's 80th birthday in 1959 was marked with a lunch party at King's, attended by several of his Bloomsbury friends including Leonard Woolf and Vanessa Bell. His 90th birthday was celebrated by a chapel concert. He died aged 91 in 1971. (*Reproduced by permission of the Provost & Fellows of King's College, Cambridge*)

E.M. Forster and Christopher Isherwood were acquainted, and are photographed here probably in Forster's rooms in King's College. Isherwood studied history at Corpus Christi from 1923 but was a devotee of I.A. Richards, the inspiring literary critic and author of *Practical Criticism*. Isherwood's autobiography *Lions and Shadows* depicts Cambridge as a surreal and threatening place. (*Reproduced by permission of the Provost & Fellows of King's College, Cambridge*)

The gateway of St John's College, *c*. 1900. St John's College was founded in 1511 by the will of Lady Margaret, Countess of Richmond and Derby and mother of Henry VII. It is Cambridge's second largest college and has impressive literary alumni, including the Tudor poet Sir Thomas Wyatt (*c*. 1503–42). He arrived at St John's College in 1516 aged 12. He was a close friend of John Leland (*c*. 1506–52) and is generally thought to have helped bring Italian forms into English verse. Wyatt was unfortunate enough to have been named as one of the ill-fated Anne Boleyn's lovers, but although he was imprisoned in the Tower of London he escaped execution. (*Cambridgeshire Collection, Cambridge Central Library*)

St John's Great Hall possesses several fine portraits of distinguished writers, including William Wordsworth, Matthew Prior and Samuel Butler. The Wordsworth Room, now a conference venue, incorporates the small room over the kitchens which the poet occupied during his years as a sizar at the college. (*Cambridgeshire Collection, Cambridge Central Library*)

Matthew Prior (1664–1721), poet and author of *Four Dialogues of the Dead* and *Down Hall* (both 1721), was born in Wimborne and educated at Westminster School and St John's College between 1682 and 1686. He became a Fellow in 1688 but left shortly afterwards to enter the diplomatic service. He died at Wimpole Hall, just outside Cambridge, in 1721 and is buried at Westminster Abbey. (*Portrait by Alexis Simon Belle, c. 1713–14, reproduced by permission of the Masters and Fellows of St John's College, Cambridge*)

Samuel Butler (1835–1902), satirist and novelist, was born in Langar and entered St John's College in 1854. Like many men of his background he was expected after graduating to pursue a career in the Church but chose instead to emigrate to New Zealand. His travels in the country appeared first in the college magazine, *The Eagle*. His works include *Erewhon* (1872) and *The Way of All Flesh* (1903). Butler was an accomplished artist, and this is his self-portrait. (*Reproduced by permission of the Master & Fellows of St John's College, Cambridge*)

William Wordsworth was brought to Cambridge in October 1787 by his uncle the Revd William Cookson. He was a 'sizar', which meant that he was required to carry out certain college tasks. He was given a tiny room above the kitchens on F staircase, about which he wrote in *The Prelude*, III, 46–50:

> The Evangelist St. John my patron was:
> Three Gothic courts are his, and in the first
> Was my abiding-place, a nook obscure;
> Right underneath, the College kitchens made
> A humming sound, less tuneable than bees . . .

(Portrait by Henry William Pickersgill, c. 1831, reproduced by permission of the Master & Fellows of St John's College, Cambridge)

St John's old chapel ruins. (*Cambridgeshire Collection, Cambridge Central Library*)

This is the chapel the young Wordsworth would have known. It was demolished in the late nineteenth century, when this photograph was taken. Initially Wordsworth found the competitive atmosphere unsettling. Despite this, in his first term he came first and, having secured a Founder's Scholarship, became very enamoured of student life. In *The Prelude*, III, 30–45, he writes:

> ' . . . I roamed
> Delighted through the motley spectacle;
> Gown grave, or gaudy, doctors, students, streets,
> Courts, cloisters, flocks of churches, gateways, towers:
> Migration strange for a stripling of the hills,
> A northern villager.

The new chapel at St John's College Chapel. Wordsworth rebelled against the requirement to attend church twice a day. He found his religion in nature and the lives of great men. He read a huge amount of his predecessors' poetry. Their presence in the city influenced him greatly: (*Cambridgeshire Collection, Cambridge Central Library*)

> Ground where the grass had yielded to the steps
> Of generations of illustrious men,
> Unmoved. I could not always lightly pass
> Through the same gateways, sleep where they had slept,
> Wake where they waked, range that inclosure old,
> That garden of great intellects, undisturbed.
>
> *The Prelude*, III, 258–64

> Beside the pleasant Mill of Trumpington
> I laughed with Chaucer; in the hawthorn shade;
> Heard him, while birds were warbling, tell his tales
> Of amorous passion. And that gentle Bard,
> Chosen by the Muses for their Page of State –
> Sweet Spenser, moving through his clouded heaven
> With the moon's beauty and the moon's soft pace,
> I called him Brother, Englishman, and Friend!
> Yea, our blind Poet, who, in his later day,
> Stood almost single; uttering odious truth . . .
>
> *The Prelude*, III, 275–92

St John's College – Bridge of Sighs. On 27 January 1791 Wordsworth was awarded a pass degree without honours and left the university. His brother Christopher remained in the city longer, eventually becoming Master of Trinity College in 1820. William returned to Cambridge many times to visit Christopher, often with his wife Mary and sister Dorothy. (*Cambridgeshire Collection, Cambridge Central Library*)

Visiting Cambridge and his old college again in December 1830, as an established poet, Wordsworth was impressed by a 'respectable show of poetry' and noted that the abilities of 'Two brothers of the name of Tennyson, in particular, are not a little promising'. (*Cambridgeshire Collection, Cambridge Central Library*)

3

Inspired by a Cambridge College

Selwyn College.
(Cambridgeshire Collection, Cambridge Central Library)

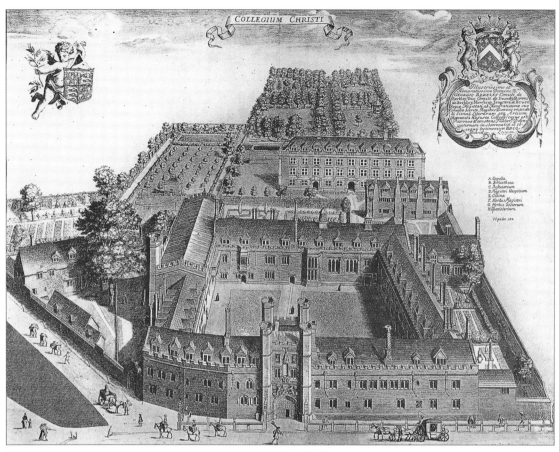

John Milton (1608–74) came up to Christ's College in 1625 and remained in residence until receiving his MA in 1632. Milton was a gentle, pale and serious student and his dedication to his work earned him the nickname 'Domina', the 'lady' of Christ's. He was critical of the academic regime, which he found 'medieval'. Dr Johnson tells of an incident where Milton was subjected to corporal punishment by his tutor William Chappell. He was also rusticated in March 1626. Milton was a Puritan and vehement anti-Royalist, which set him apart from many of his college companions.

It was at Christ's, however, that Milton became friends with Edward King, who was the inspiration behind *Lycidas* (1638). John Cleveland (1613–58), one of Milton's contemporaries, also penned an elegy to King.

In 'An Apology for Smectymnuus' Milton describes his Cambridge days, writing of the 'more than ordinary favour and respect which I found above any of my equals at the hands of those courteous and learned men, the Fellowes of that Colledge wherein I spent some yeares'.

His most famous writings include *Paradise Lost*. The manuscript of *Lycidas* is kept by Trinity College, and the University Library houses many others. (*Reproduced by permission of the Master and Fellows of Christ's College, Cambridge*)

Opposite, top: An engraving of Christ's College, *c.* 1810. Originally established as 'God's House' in 1437, Christ's College was officially founded by Henry VI in 1448. Lady Margaret Beaufort, mother of Henry VII, re-founded it as Christ's College in 1505. Christ's literary alumni include John Milton (1608–74) and John Leland. Leland, who graduated in 1522, was Henry VIII's archivist and claimed to have preserved many important literary manuscripts from monasteries at the time of the dissolution. The library of Christ's contains numerous Anglo-Saxon manuscripts (mostly donated by Archbishop Parker) including the *Anglo-Saxon Chronicle*. (*Cambridgeshire Collection, Cambridge Central Library*)

Opposite, bottom: Christ's College gateway. (*Cambridgeshire Collection, Cambridge Central Library*)

Milton had rooms in First Court at Christ's during his time as a student (1625–32). Local wisdom says he occupied rooms just to the left of the entrance gateway on staircase M3. It was here that Wordsworth, overwhelmed by the literary association, drank his first and last alcohol in a toast to the poet. Milton wrote 'Hymn on the Morning of Christ's Nativity' (1629) and other poems while living here, including verses on Thomas Hobson, the Cambridge carrier who hired out horses in strict rotation, so giving rise to the term Hobson's choice. Milton's reflections on the University are recorded in 'Il Penseroso' 1632:

> But let my due feet never fail
> To walk the studious cloister's pale,
> And love the high embowed roof,
> With antique pillars massy proof,
> And storied windows richly dight
> Casting a dim religious light.

In the Fellows' Garden is Milton's mulberry tree, supposedly planted by Milton during his student days. There is no evidence linking Milton with this mulberry tree but it was probably growing at Christ's during his time there and is said to be the only survivor of a group of the species planted in 1608 to feed colonies of silk worms.

The bathing pool near here is fed by fresh water from Hobson's Conduit. Among the busts that line the edge is one of Milton (there is another in the Senior Combination room at Christ's), and to the east side is an urn containing the ashes of C.P. Snow (1905–80), a Fellow of Christ's from 1930 to 1950. Snow wrote an eleven-volume sequence of novels, *Strangers and Brothers*, of which three are set in Cambridge.

Colin Dexter, author of the Inspector Morse novels, set in Oxford and now adapted into a series of TV programmes, graduated from Christ's College in 1950. He has won numerous awards including the Crime Writers Association Silver, Gold and Diamond Dagger awards, the latter for outstanding services to crime literature. In 1999 Dexter wrote of his Cambridge years: 'I felt – feel – extremely privileged to get in. . . . What I recall most is meeting so many fellow undergraduates who were so much brighter and so much more knowledgeable than I was. I had my foot hard down on the accelerator whilst they coasted along in some fifth gear.' (*Cambridgeshire Collection, Cambridge Central Library*)

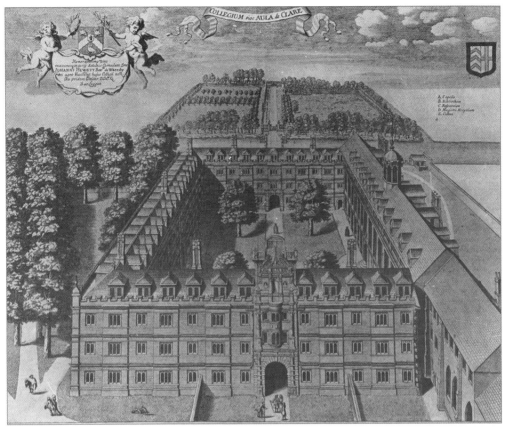

An engraving of Clare College. Founded in 1326 and so one of the University's oldest colleges, Clare College is also one of its most beautiful. Its elegant courts are perfectly complemented by the most wonderful gardens. Clare is one of the colleges proposed for Soler Hall (described by Chaucer in *The Reeve's Tale*). (*Cambridgeshire Collection, Cambridge Central Library*)

Clare Bridge – looking towards the Backs. Situated on the river and central to the city, Clare College lies behind the Old Schools building near King's College Chapel, crosses the river, runs down to the Backs and up to the University Library. (*Cambridgeshire Collection, Cambridge Central Library*)

Siegfried Sassoon (1886–1967), one of the First World War's most famous poets, entered Clare College in 1905 to read Law and then History. Cambridge had a long-lasting effect upon his romantic imagination, and, like others before him, he spent many hours musing on the poets who had walked the city streets and college courts, particularly Tennyson and Edward Fitzgerald. He began to write poetry while an undergraduate here. The academic environment he found less conducive, and having failed to win the Chancellor's Medal with his poem on Edward I he left the University. *(Painting by Glyn Philpot, c. 1917, Mary Evans Picture Library)*

Clare College seen from the Backs. In 1917 Siegfried Sassoon exposed the desperation and terror of life in the trenches of the First World War in his first book of war poems, *The Old Huntsman*. He also returned his Military Cross – awarded for bravery in the face of enemy fire – and condemned the war (having already submitted several anti-war poems including 'To Any Dead Officer' to the *Cambridge Magazine*). Only the intervention of his friend, the writer Robert Graves, saved him from a court martial. He was sent to Edinburgh to be treated for 'shell shock' by the noted Cambridge psychologist W.H.R. Rivers. There he befriended fellow poet Wilfred Owen (who died at the Front in 1918). Sassoon returned to the war, and was one of the few war poets to survive. His *Collected Poems 1908–1956* was published in 1961, and he died in 1967. (*Cambridgeshire Collection, Cambridge Central Library*)

Corpus Christi College: the memorial plaque to Marlowe and Fletcher. A royal licence permitting the foundation of Corpus Christi College by the people of Cambridge was granted in 1352, and the building of Old Court began. At first the rooms were sparse, with bare walls and clay floors on the ground floor. Fellows and students slept in the same rooms.

By the time the playwrights Christopher Marlowe and John Fletcher were in residence the windows had been fully glazed, the walls wainscotted and college accommodation rendered a little more comfortable. Marlowe (1564–93) had rooms on P staircase, while John Fletcher (1579–1625) had rooms on O staircase. Fletcher formed a successful playwriting partnership with Francis Beaumont. (*Author*)

This portrait, by an unknown artist, is believed to be that of the playwright and undergraduate of Corpus Christi College, Christopher Marlowe (1564–93). The picture was discovered in the early 1950s, dirty and punctured by nails, in builders' rubble. The Latin inscription endorses the attribution to Marlowe. He would have been 21 in 1585 and was still in residence at Corpus Christi at the time. The motto reads 'Quod me nutrit me destruit' ('What nourishes me destroys me'). The sitter's rich attire is intriguing (Marlowe was the son of a shoemaker) and lends weight to the rumours that Marlowe was a government spy, paid to betray students with Catholic sympathies. He achieved his BA in 1584 but chose to remain in residence, graduating with an MA in 1587. His MA was at first withheld owing to Marlowe's apparent Catholic sympathies and, intriguingly, the Privy Council intervened on his behalf to ensure it was bestowed.

Marlowe is famous as the author of *Tamburlaine* (1590: mostly written during Marlowe's student years) and *The Tragedy of Dr Faustus*. Academic argument still persists about whether he may have been the true author of some works attributed to Shakespeare. He was a very well-known dramatist in his own lifetime. Marlowe died in strange circumstances, stabbed to death in a Deptford inn in the company of men who were in the employ of Francis Walsingham, Elizabeth I's spymaster. *(Reproduced by permission of the Master and Fellows of Corpus Christi College, Cambridge. The College cannot vouchsafe for the identity of the portrait)*

Darwin College was founded in 1964, the first college exclusively for graduate students. It is in the heart of the city and was named in honour of the Darwin family. Charles Darwin, son of the eminent biologist, was Plumian Professor of Astronomy at Cambridge from 1883 and bought Newnham Grange (above), now the oldest part of the college, in 1885. Literary names connected with the college include Gwen Darwin, later Raverat, who spent her childhood at Newnham Grange, in the company of her cousin Frances Darwin, later Cornford. (*Cambridgeshire Collection, Cambridge Central Library*)

Emmanuel College was founded in 1584 on the site of a priory of the Dominican Order, known as the Black Friars. The chapel was designed by Sir Christopher Wren.

In the 1630s many Puritan clergy fled England for the New England colonies of America to avoid persecution. It is said that many of these men came from Emmanuel College and one of them, John Harvard (BA 1632), gave his name to the first American university. Famous literary alumni include the critic F.R. Leavis and the novelist Sir Hugh Walpole (1884–1941) – an undergraduate at Emmanuel between 1902 and 1905. (*Cambridgeshire Collection, Cambridge Central Library*)

A room in Emmanuel College. Dr Samuel Johnson (1709–84) made one recorded visit to Cambridge, on 16 February 1765, in the company of the Hon. Topham Beauclerk. They stopped at the Rose from Saturday until Tuesday. Johnson was by this time a very well-known literary figure and attempted to be as anonymous as possible on his travels. He was in the city to see his old friend the Shakespeare scholar and Fellow of Emmanuel College Dr Richard Farmer. Together they saw Trinity Library, dined at Sidney Sussex and enjoyed evening recitals and robust argument. (*Cambridgeshire Collection, Cambridge Central Library*)

Sir Christopher Wren's chapel can be seen upon entering Emmanuel College. It shows the influence of other chapels of Wren's design in Cambridge, notably at Peterhouse and Pembroke.

In the Fellows' Garden beyond this court is a great oriental plane tree, unusual for its 'weeping' pose. It is thought to have been planted in about 1835 and was noticed by the exiled Spanish poet Luis Cernuda (1902–63), a resident of Emmanuel College during the Second World War. It appears in his poem 'El árbol'. (*Cambridgeshire Collection, Cambridge Central Library*)

Above: Gonville and Caius College, *c.* 1890. The college, founded in 1348, is at the heart of the city very near Senate House, looks out to Great St Mary's and runs back along Trinity Street. Charles Doughty (1843–1926), author of *Travels in Arabia Deserta* (1888), studied here from 1861 to 1863. This work is said to have had a profound effect on T.E Lawrence, later better known as 'Lawrence of Arabia' and author of *Seven Pillars of Wisdom.* (*Cambridgeshire Collection, Cambridge Central Library*)

Jesus College gatehouse, *c.* 1880. Jesus is the most intriguing of Cambridge colleges. It was founded in 1496 and built among the distinctive ruins of a twelfth-century Benedictine nunnery. It now has a reputation for artistry and the gardens are filled with beautiful and unusual modern sculptures. Famous literary alumni include Laurence Sterne (1713–68), Samuel Taylor Coleridge (1772–1834), the novelist Nick Hornby, radio correspondent Alastair Cooke, Sir Arthur Quiller-Couch, playwright David Hare, poet and biographer Robert Gittings, literary critic Lisa Jardine and the influential left-wing writer and critic Raymond Williams. (*Cambridgeshire Collection, Cambridge Central Library*)

Jesus College: the Burne-Jones window. The chapel was restored in 1844. The pavement and stalls are the work of Augustus Pugin, who worked on the Houses of Parliament. In 1867 the nave was given a new ceiling, designed by William Morris, and in 1873 its windows were glazed with patterns by Edward Burne-Jones under the direction of Morris.

Alastair Cooke (1908–2004; Jesus 1927), 'Britain's favourite American', surveyed the world from his armchair overlooking Central Park in New York (where he recorded his weekly 'Letter from America'). In his second year at Cambridge he founded 'The Mummers' dramatic group which still exists and which scandalised the University by being the first society to allow women to act on stage. (*Cambridgeshire Collection, Cambridge Central Library*)

Cloisters at Jesus College. The Senior Combination room and college dining room display portraits of Samuel Taylor Coleridge, Laurence Sterne and Sir Arthur Quiller-Couch.

Coleridge was the son of a deceased clergyman and as such qualified for a Rustat scholarship to the College. Despite this support he soon fell into debt and later became an opium addict. Coleridge was influenced significantly by his tutor, William Frend, who converted him to Unitarianism and who was something of an agitator. Coleridge left Jesus in December 1793 and joined the 15th Regiment of Light Dragoons under an assumed name – Silas Tomkyn Comberbache. He was bought out of service two months later and returned to Jesus College but never actually took his degree. The Old Library houses a number of pieces of Coleridge memorabilia, including several manuscripts and a curl of his hair.

In *Biographia Literaria* (1817) he recalls his Cambridge years: 'friendly cloisters, and the happy grove of quiet, ever honoured Jesus College'. The chapel carries a memorial to him. (*Cambridgeshire Collection, Cambridge Central Library*)

Jesus College – the gatehouse at the turn of century. Laurence Sterne arrived at Jesus in 1733, where he met John Hall, his friend and inspiration for his depiction of *Eugenius*. Laurence Sterne was a descendant of Richard Sterne (who was imprisoned by Cromwell) and entered Jesus College on a scholarship endowed by his forebear. His academic career was, however, inhibited by his poverty and after graduation he lived in considerable debt for many years. He is best known as the author of *The Life and Opinions of Tristram Shandy* (1760–7). (*Cambridgeshire Collection, Cambridge Central Library*)

The Pepysian Library.

Published by J. W. Puckering, West Strand.

The Pepys Library. The site of Magdalene College was originally a Benedictine hostel. It was refounded as a university college in 1542. It has two libraries, the world-famous Pepys Library and the Old Library. (*Cambridgeshire Collection, Cambridge Central Library*)

Magdalene's most famous son, Samuel Pepys (1633–1703), is famous for his diary, which provides a fascinating description of life in seventeenth-century England. Pepys arrived in Cambridge in 1651 as an undergraduate of Trinity Hall. However, he quickly elected to move to Magdalene College, probably in search of a scholarship.

Pepys wrote in his diary of 31 December 1664: 'Went to reside in Magd. Coll. Cambridge, and put on my gown first March 5 1651.' While there he learnt his diary shorthand – tachygraphy – which would perplex later scholars of his work. Pepys enjoyed the sociability of college life and became a friend of John Dryden. He tried his hand at playwriting and penned *Love a Cheat*. In 1654 he gained his degree and moved back to London.

In the diary, which he began on 1 January 1660 and ceased in 1669, he records several trips to Cambridge. In February 1660 while visiting his brother John he stayed at the Falcon Inn (now demolished) in Petty Cury, the Three Tuns and the Rose Inn (in Rose Crescent) near Market Hill. In October 1662, when elected to his MA, Pepys stayed at The Bear (which was located near Market Passage).

Five years later, after he had witnessed the Great Fire, escaped the plague and become a man of status, Pepys returned again:

> . . . away to Cambridge, it being foul, rainy weather; and there did take up at the Rose . . . took my wife and W. Hewer and Willett . . . and showed them Trinity College and St John's Library, and went to King's College Chapel to see the outside of it only, and so to our Inne; and with much pleasure did this, they walking in their pretty morning gowns, very handsome, and I proud to find myself in condition to do this.

(Portrait reproduced by permission of the Master & Fellows of Magdalene College, Cambridge)

The exterior of the Pepys Library. The Pepys Library houses the diarist's complete library, arranged by height, in cases of his own design. (*Reproduced by permission of the Master & Fellows of Magdalene College, Cambridge*)

The interior of the Pepys Library. The inscription 'Bibliotheca Pepysiana 1724' above the entrance notes the date when Pepys's personal collection was installed in the College. Pepys's coat of arms and his motto '*Mens cujusque is est quisque*' ('The mind's the man') are painted above this frieze.

Pepys spent a great deal of money collecting his impressive library of 3,000 volumes and in 1703 he left it all to his nephew John Jackson, on the condition that following John's death it would go to a university college. John chose Magdalene and rooms Pepys had helped to build. The books were bound with Pepys's crest and arms on each cover and arranged, as they are to this day, in twelve bookcases or 'oak presses' with glass doors. The six volumes of Pepys's diary, all written in shorthand, were presented to the library in 1819. It took one man, John Smith, three years to transcribe them, without the aid of the tachygraphy book which was in Pepys's library! Sir Walter Scott reviewed them. A full version edited by Robert Latham and William Matthews began publication in the 1970s. (*Reproduced by permission of the Master & Fellows of Magdalene College, Cambridge*)

First Court, Magdalene College, *c.* 1900. C.S. Lewis (1898–1963) became a Fellow of Magdalene College in 1954, when he came to Cambridge from Oxford to take up the post of Professor of Medieval and Renaissance Literature. Magdalene was his home during his marriage to Joy Gresham (seventeen years his junior, she died in 1960), while she remained in Oxford. They met at weekends and holidays. Lewis was a forthright person, incredibly well read and in possession of a formidable intellect, which he could apply to literature of all kinds, from well-loved children's stories such as the Chronicles of Narnia to the witty *Screwtape Letters* (1942). During his tenure here he published *The Magician's Nephew* (1955), *Studies in Words*, (1960) and *An Experiment in Criticism* (1961). He died here in 1963, and is buried in Oxford. (*Cambridgeshire Collection, Cambridge Central Library*)

Benson Court, Magdalene College, *c.* 1910. A.C. Benson (1862–1925) was a prolific writer, producing over a hundred works. *From a College Window* was published in 1906 while he was a fellow of Magdalene. The author of the words for Elgar's 'Land of Hope and Glory', he became Master of Magdalene College in 1915. He is responsible for the creation of the Honorary Artistic Fellowship which Rudyard Kipling, T.S. Eliot and Thomas Hardy subsequently held. His huge collection of books formed the foundation of the English Faculty Library.

Other famous alumni include the actor Sir Michael Redgrave, author and academic Professor C.S. Lewis and literary critic Professor I.A. Richards. (*Cambridgeshire Collection, Cambridge Central Library*)

Magdalene's Honorary Artistic Fellows Kipling, Eliot and Hardy each donated manuscripts to the college, and their portraits hang in the Hall.

   T.S. Eliot (1888–1965), Oxford graduate, poet, critic and author of the highly influential *The Wasteland* (1922), *Murder in the Cathedral* (1935) and *Four Quartets* (1944), gave the 1926 Clark Lectures at Cambridge. Despite repeated requests Eliot never took up the offer to become a don. (*Portrait of T.S. Eliot by Wyndham Lewis, 1949, reproduced by permission of the Master & Fellows of Magdalene College*)

A portrait of Thomas Hardy (1840–1928), by R.E. Fuller Maitland. Hardy's poem 'Standing by the mantelpiece' is said to have been written in June 1873, during a visit to his friend Horace Moule, then resident in Queens' College. Moule showed Hardy King's College Chapel and together they climbed to the roof to see Ely Cathedral.

Hardy returned to Cambridge again in October 1880 with his wife Emma, following Moule's suicide, an event which affected him considerably. He came again in 1909 and then in 1913 to receive an honorary doctorate and honorary fellowship at Magdalene College. (*Reproduced by permission of the Master & Fellows of Magdalene College, Cambridge*)

A portrait of Rudyard Kipling (1865–1936). Kipling, a Fellow of Magdalene College, poet and novelist, was a frequent visitor to Cambridge. His most well-known works include *Barrack Room Ballads* (1892) and the *Just So Stories* (1902). (*Reproduced by permission of the Master & Fellows of Magdalene College, Cambridge*)

Charles Kingsley (1819–75) was an undergraduate at Magdalene from 1838 to 1842 and became Professor of Modern History in 1860. His novel *Alton Locke* (1850) is set partly in Cambridge. He is best known for his works *The Water Babies* (1863), *Westward Ho!* (1855) and *Hereward the Wake* (1866). (*Cambridgeshire Collection, Cambridge Central Library*)

Pembroke College, with a view of the Chapel and Library. Pembroke College was founded in 1374 by Mary de Saint Paul, widow of the earl of Pembroke, and is one of the university's oldest colleges. The Chapel was designed by Sir Christopher Wren and the Library has manuscripts written by Gray, including 'Elegy in a Country Churchyard'. In the hall there is a portrait of Edward Spenser (1552–99), author of *The Faerie Queene* (1590). Richard Crashaw was a student between 1632 and 1634 as was Thomas Gray. More recent alumni include Peter Cook, Poet Laureate Ted Hughes, Clive James, Eric Idle and Tom Sharpe who for many years lived on Mill Road. His portrait of an elitist Cambridge college in *Porterhouse Blue* (1974) is extremely funny. (*Cambridgeshire Collection, Cambridge Central Library*)

A view of the dining hall in Pembroke College. During the seventeenth century and the English Civil War Pembroke was home to a number of Royalist poets, including the mystic Richard Crashaw (1612–49) and Gabriel Harvey (c. 1545–1630).

In the eighteenth century the Ivy Court was built to the east of the Hall and it was here that the poet Thomas Gray moved in 1756. Gray (1716–71) had been a scholar at Peterhouse but found the atmosphere there unsettling and soon made Pembroke his home, remaining there for the rest of his life. The inspiration for his most famous work, 'Elegy written in a Country Churchyard' (1751), has been attributed to the church in Grantchester, but a little church in Stoke Poges, Buckinghamshire, is the more likely candidate. Gray's rooms in the corner of Ivy Court were occupied in 1773 by William Pitt the Younger, who later became the youngest Prime Minister in British history.

Edmund Spenser (1552–99), author of *The Faerie Queene*, was a precocious poet, having penned *Hymnes in honour of Love and Beauty* before his arrival at Pembroke College, which he entered as a sizar in 1569. He graduated in 1573. He was firm friends with Gabriel Harvey, who helped to secure him the patronage of the Earl of Leicester, and a contemporary of Robert Greene, the poet and pamphleteer (1560–92). In Book IV, Canto XI, stanza 34 of *The Faerie Queene*, he writes of the city:

> My mother Cambridge, whom as with a Crowne
> He doth adorne, and is adorn'd of it
> With many a gentle Muse and many a learned wit.

Edward James (Ted) Hughes (1930–98) entered Pembroke College with an Open Exhibition in English, but later switched to read Archaeology and Anthropology. He continued to contribute poems to Cambridge magazines after he left, many of them having international circulation and the support of many influential subscribers. The story of the life, marriages and poetry of Ted Hughes is well known and detailed later in this book. He was Poet Laureate from 1985 until his death in 1998. (*Cambridgeshire Collection, Cambridge Central Library*)

Opposite, bottom: Ivy Court, Pembroke College. In his book *May Week was in June*, Clive James describes the impact of Cambridge upon him: 'I had landed in the lap of the only kind of luxury I had ever cared about – a wealth of opportunity.' (*Cambridgeshire Collection, Cambridge Central Library*)

A portrait of Christopher Smart. Smart (1722–71) came up to Pembroke in 1742 as a Classics scholar. His university career was decidedly mixed; he was extravagant and wilful and neglected to mention to the college authorities that he was married. His play *A Trip to Cambridge* was ill-received, notably by his contemporary at Peterhouse, Thomas Gray, but his success in the Seatonian Prize (a prestigious university writing competition) saved him on two occasions from the wrath of his creditors. Christopher Smart penned 'The Jubilee Ode' in celebration of the college's fourth centenary while he was a student at Pembroke in 1743. He became a Fellow in 1745 but left Cambridge in 1755 for London where he worked as a journalist and kept company with Dr Johnson (1709–84) and Oliver Goldsmith (*c*. 1730–74), poet, playwright and novelist. In 1756 he was committed to an asylum where his rather idiosyncratic poetry flourished. (*Getty Images*)

Thomas Gray's room in Peterhouse. Gray was an undergraduate at Peterhouse from 1734 to 1738 and also in residence in Cambridge from 1743 to 1756. Gray had a morbid fear of fire and it is still possible to see the fire escape bar on the window of his former rooms in the college. Gray went to Pembroke from nearby Peterhouse, and became Professor of History and Modern Languages in 1768. He took rooms in the Hitcham Building in the Second Court, living there from 1756 until his death in 1771. In 'Ode to Music' (1769) Gray writes of the 'Willowy Camus' and 'the cloister dim', and his *Letters* show that he preferred the city and the colleges when people left them to themselves. *(Author)*

A watercolour of Peterhouse, *c.* 1890. Peterhouse was founded in 1284 by Hugh Balsham, Bishop of Ely and is the oldest and smallest of the Cambridge colleges. It retains the old form 'house or hall'.

John Skelton is thought to have been a member of the college, graduating in 1484. In 1493 he was honoured with the title Poet Laureate. Richard Crashaw, poet and Fellow of Peterhouse, was expelled in 1643 for refusing to accept the Solemn League and Covenant. Sam Mendes was a student at Peterhouse from 1984 until 1987 reading English. In 2000 he won an Academy Award as Best Director for the film *American Beauty.* (*Cambridgeshire Collection, Cambridge Central Library*)

Peterhouse Deer Park. In early November 1885 Henry Currie Marillier, a student at Peterhouse and a friend of Oscar Wilde (1854–1900), wrote inviting him to a performance of *Eumenides*. Wilde arrived in Cambridge on 27 November and was richly entertained by the students there. Marillier, Wilde and another student, J.H. Bradley, talked of poetry. Wilde dismissed Bradley's favourite, Shelley, proclaiming Keats to be the greatest of the poets. When Wilde left Cambridge he was walked to the station by a group of young men. He later wrote of his visit, 'I remember bright young faces, and grey misty quadrangles . . . and, what I love best in the world, Poetry and Paradox dancing together!' (*Cambridgeshire Collection, Cambridge Central Library*)

Old Court, Queens' College. The apostrophe in Queens' College owes its place to the fact that the college was founded twice, by different English queens, by Margaret of Anjou in 1448 and in 1465 by Elizabeth Woodville. The college lies along the banks of the Cam. The Old Court dates from 1448 and is one of the finest and best preserved examples of a medieval court in England. Queens' literary alumni include novelists, playwrights, comics and others.

Dr John Hall obtained an MA from Queens' in 1597 and then studied on the continent to complete his medical training. He set up a practice in Stratford-upon-Avon and in 1607 married William Shakespeare's eldest daughter, Susannah, in Holy Trinity Church. Hall's patients included the poet Michael Drayton (1563–1631) and his own father-in-law. Although there is no record of Drayton visiting Cambridge it features regularly in his work. Song XXI of his countrywide survey, *Poly-Olbion* (1622), concerns Ely and Cambridge:

> O noble *Cambridge* then, my most beloved Towne,
> In glory flourish still, to heighten thy renowne . . .

(Cambridgeshire Collection, Cambridge Central Library)

Left: The Erasmus Tower at Queens' College. Desiderius Erasmus (*c.* 1466–1536), the humanist, eminent writer, scholar and wit, is reputed to have stayed at Queens' College in the sixteenth century, living in rooms in Erasmus Tower (Pump Court, which looks over Silver Street) between 1511 and 1514 while the first Lady Margaret Reader in Greek. In his letters to friends he frequently complains about the discomfort of the city and although there is no written evidence for his occupancy of these rooms it is highly likely. His *Letters and Colloquia* have proven fertile sources of inspiration for other writers. (*Cambridgeshire Collection, Cambridge Central Library*)

Below: Queens' College and the Mathematical Bridge. T.H. White's novel *Darkness at Pemberley* is set in a thinly disguised Queens' College. Graham Swift (Queens' 1967–70), novelist and Booker Prize-winner, was born in 1949 and entered Queens' College in 1967. His most successful work, *Waterland*, draws on Swift's encounters with the Fens during his time in Cambridge. (*Cambridgeshire Collection, Cambridge Central Library*)

St Catherine's College, *c.* 1880. The college was founded in 1473 by Robert Wodelarke, then Provost of neighbouring King's College.

James Shirley, author of the poem 'Narcissus' (first published as 'Eccho'), came to St Catherine's from Oxford and graduated in 1618. Malcolm Lowry (1909–57), novelist and short-story writer, came to the college from The Leys School in the town and was an undergraduate from 1929 to 1932. He was close friends with Charlotte Haldane and Conrad Aiken. His novel *Ultramarine* (1933) was, rather unusually, accepted by his tutor in lieu of a thesis. The actor Ian McKellen and the journalist and political commentator Jeremy Paxman are also old boys, as is Sir Peter Hall (1951), former Director of the Royal Shakespeare Company, The National Theatre and Glyndebourne. (*Cambridgeshire Collection, Cambridge Central Library*)

A late eighteenth-century watercolour of Sidney Sussex College. Founded by Lady Frances Sidney, Countess of Sussex in 1596, Sidney Sussex College lies in the heart of the city and yet possesses a very peaceful atmosphere. Sidney Sussex is one of the colleges identified as the Alma Mater of the legendary Sherlock Holmes. The crime writer Dorothy L. Sayers was convinced that Sir Arthur Conan Doyle left clues indicating this in the stories. Less fictional alumni include Thomas Rymer, critic and author of *A Short View of Tragedy* (1692).

No consideration of Sidney Sussex would be complete without mention of Oliver Cromwell, whose political writings earned him a place here and whose head, rather gruesomely, is rumoured to be buried in a secret location in the college. Cromwell was a huge influence on Marvell, Milton and Dryden, who wrote in great depth about his life and career. (*Cambridgeshire Collection, Cambridge Central Library*)

Trinity Hall was founded in 1350 on a pretty river-site in the heart of the city. It nestles between Clare College and Trinity College.

Thomas Preston, author of *Cambises, King of Persia* (1569), became a Fellow of King's in 1556 and went on to be Master of Trinity Hall. Edward Bulwer Lytton won the Chancellor's Medal in 1825 for his poem 'Sculpture'. J.B. Priestley (1894–1984) also studied at the college. (*Cambridgeshire Collection, Cambridge Central Library*)

Leslie Stephen (1832–1904), father of Virginia Woolf, was an undergraduate at Trinity Hall between 1850 and 1854, and a Fellow until 1867. In his work *Life*, published in 1885, he tells the reader that Mr Henry James believes the Fellows' Garden to be unsurpassed in Europe, and quotes him as saying: 'If I were called upon to mention the prettiest corner of the world, I should draw a thoughtful sigh and point the way to the gardens of Trinity Hall.' (*Cambridgeshire Collection, Cambridge Central Library*)

4

Cambridge Women

Girls in room – a photo from the beginning of the twentieth century.
(*Cambridgeshire Collection, Cambridge Central Library*)

'In Cambridge and the plays of Ibsen alone does it seem appropriate for the heroine before the great crises of life to enter, take off her overshoes, and put her wet umbrella upon the writing desk.'

H.G. Wells

King's College. Celia Fiennes (1662–1741), the famous lady diarist who travelled the length and breadth of England side-saddle, visited Cambridge in 1697. She greatly admired the Wren Library at Trinity College, and the recently landscaped Backs with their pretty bridges and elegant walks. Rather intrepidly, she climbed to the roof of King's College Chapel. (*Cambridgeshire Collection, Cambridge Central Library*)

Rooms within the grounds of Newnham College. (*Cambridgeshire Collection, Cambridge Central Library*)

P.D. James must have had a similar scene in mind when she wrote the following:

But now by what devious routes and for what a strange purpose she had come at last to Cambridge. The city didn't disappoint her. In her wanderings she had seen lovelier places, but none in which she had been happier or more at peace. How indeed, she thought, could the heart be indifferent to such a city where stone and stained glass, water and green lawns, trees and flowers were arranged in such ordered beauty for the service of learning.

P.D. James, *An Unsuitable Job for a Woman*

Newnham College was founded in 1871 to enable women to receive a Cambridge education. At that time they were not entitled to receive University of Cambridge degrees. The first Principal of the college was Miss Anne Clough (right).

Jane Harrison (1850–1928) was one of the first to be educated at Newnham College. She was a very talented student of archaeology and religion and a driving force behind the Marlowe Society and Rupert Brooke's 'Neo-Pagans'. She is thought to be 'J.H.' in Virginia Woolf's *A Room of One's Own*. Among the impressive literary alumni of Newnham are A.S. Byatt, Margaret Drabble and Sylvia Plath. (*Cambridgeshire Collection, Cambridge Central Library*)

Mrs Sidgwick, the college Principal from 1892 to 1911. On 24 October 1878 the Russian novelist Ivan Sergeyevich Turgenev (1813–83), author of *Fathers and Sons* (1862), was driven to Cambridge by Henry Sidgwick on 24 October 1878. He had lunch at 18 Brookside and was then taken to see Newnham College by Mrs Sidgwick. (*Cambridgeshire Collection, Cambridge Central Library*)

Anti-women day at Cambridge, 1897. After two months of national debate, degree titles were again refused to women students, male undergraduates rejecting the idea of offering women membership of the University by 2,137 to 298. On 21 May, the day of the formal vote, the city was awash with anti-women banners. The vote refused women degrees by 1,707 to 661. The triumphant male establishment rampaged through the streets to Newnham. Thwarted by barred gates they set up a bonfire in Market Square.

The men of the university actively campaigned to exclude women from gaining formal university qualifications. This photo shows the strength of anti-women feeling. 'Nasty forward minxes,' exclaimed the geologist Adam Sedgwick on being told that girls had been admitted to Cambridge Local Examinations in 1864.

Sir Arthur Quiller-Couch became a Fellow of Jesus College in 1912 when he was elected Professor of English Literature. His published lectures, *On the Art of Writing* (1916) and *On the Art of Reading* (1920), were highly influential in Cambridge and beyond. His habit of ignoring the female students in his lectures or addressing them as 'Sir', however, did not endear him at Girton or Newnham Colleges. (*Cambridgeshire Collection, Cambridge Central Library*)

A portrait of Virginia Woolf (1882–1941) by Man Ray. Arguably the twentieth century's most innovative novelist, Virginia Woolf was a regular visitor to Cambridge, where her brother Thoby Stephen (1880–1906) was an undergraduate at Trinity College. Their father Leslie Stephen (a student at Trinity Hall in the 1850s) wrote, in his *Essay On Coleridge*, of 'Cambridge, the mother of Poets . . .' and it can certainly be viewed as the mother of the Bloomsbury Group, the bohemian collective that was to influence generations by living a new intellectual and social movement – Modernism.

It was on a May Week afternoon in Thoby's rooms that Leonard Woolf first met Virginia Stephen. He described how her beauty took his breath away though it was to be ten years before they married, during which time Virginia was proposed to by Lytton Strachey (1880–1932), the biographer and author of *Eminent Victorians* (1918). Many believe it was Virginia's influence that ensured the importance of the Bloomsbury Group to the cultural world beyond Cambridge.

Her cousin Katherine Stephen was at this time Vice-President of Newnham College and she often stayed with her Aunt Caroline 'The Quaker' Stephen at The Porch, 33 Grantchester Street. During a visit there in 1904 she wrote, 'No place in the world can be lovelier . . . Lord! How dull it would be to live here!'

In 1924 Virginia returned to lecture to the Heretics Society where she controversially maintained that strict narrative structures were confining and dispensable. In October 1928 she was called back and gave two lectures on 'Women and Fiction' to the Arts Society at Newnham and the ODTAA Society at Girton (she was accompanied by her friend, the author and poet Vita Sackville-West). Virginia described Girton's warren of corridors as 'like vaults in some horrid high church cathedral', and the women students as 'intelligent, eager, poor; and destined to become schoolmistresses in shoals'. It was from these lectures and observations that she developed her feminist masterpiece *A Room of One's Own* (1929). In the book she compares the lavish lunch of the dons at King's with the homely impoverishment of the women's colleges.

Virginia was also a close friend of the poet Rupert Brooke and worked on her novel *The Voyage Out* in his garden at Grantchester. She admired Brooke for his charisma and confidence but was less impressed by his poetry, which she described as 'all adjectives and contortions'. 'I didn't think then much of his poetry,' she wrote, 'which he read aloud on the lawn, but I thought he would be Prime Minister.' Virginia was also friends with the Darwin and Cornford families in Cambridge. *(National Portrait Gallery)*

Women students at Newnham in the late nineteenth century. Katherine Bradley (1848–1914), who in collaboration with her niece wrote as Michael Field, was one of Newnham's first students. They worked hard and received considerable support from other women in society, particularly writers such as Virginia Woolf and Vita Sackville-West.

The poet Robert Browning (1812–89) visited the city to attend a meeting of the Cambridge University Browning Society. Afterwards he was invited to Newnham College, where we are told an undergraduate offered him a crown of roses she had woven for the occasion, which he dutifully wore all through tea! *(Cambridgeshire Collection, Cambridge Central Library)*

A girl reading in her college room. Virginia Woolf's *A Room of One's Own* (1929) is the development of the lectures she gave to the Arts Society at Newnham and at the ODTAA (One Damned Thing After Another) meeting at Girton during 1928. *(Cambridgeshire Collection, Cambridge Central Library)*

George Eliot (Mary Ann Evans), a painting dated 1849, by F.D. Durade. Eliot (1819–80), author of *Silas Marner* (1861) and *Daniel Deronda* (1876) among many others, and George Henry Lewes visited Cambridge as the guests of the Vice-Master of Trinity in February 1868. They stayed at the Bull.

They returned in May 1873, this time to see F.W.H. Myers, who greatly admired the forceful novelist. He wrote of her 'grave, majestic countenance' and how profound her conversation was: '. . . the words God, Immortality, Duty . . . how inconceivable was the first, how unbelievable the second, and yet how . . . absolute the third'.

In May 1877, with Henry Sidgwick, Eliot visited the two new colleges for women, Newnham and Girton. She wrote of her time in Cambridge in *A College Breakfast Party* (1878). George Eliot was also a friend of Turgenev (1818–83), with whom she visited Newmarket. *(National Portrait Gallery)*

Newnham College Library. The novelist Rose Macaulay (1881–1958), resident in Cambridge in the 1920s, wrote *Orphan Island* in 1924, depicting everyday life in an academic household. *They Were Defeated* (1932) is based in seventeenth-century Cambridge and features Milton, Marvell, John Cleveland and Abraham Cowley.

Frances Cornford, née Darwin (1886–1960), cousin of Gwen Raverat, lived at Conduit Head near Madingley Road. Her first poetry collection was published in 1910. Cambridge features frequently in her work, especially her postwar collection *Travelling Home* (1948). Her poem 'In The Backs' is a moving recollection of the loss of her friend Rupert Brooke and her son John. It was she who described Brooke as a 'golden-haired young Apollo' in her poem 'Youth'. She was clearly taken with the poet as he appears in 'The Secret River' and 'Views and Vagabonds' (1912). Rupert Brooke called her poems 'the old, old heart-cry business'. In St Giles's Cemetery, Huntingdon Road, Cambridge there is a memorial to her.

Gwen Raverat, née Darwin (1885–1957), a granddaughter of Charles Darwin, wrote *Period Piece: A Cambridge Childhood* in 1952. The book is the tale of her childhood in Newnham Grange, Silver Street – now part of Darwin College – and offers a vivid and entertaining depiction of her Darwin family members at the turn of the last century. Both she and Frances were friends of Rose Macaulay. Gwen also fell under the spell of Rupert Brooke and his lively circle, all picnics, nude bathing and boating. She studied at the Slade School of Art in London and developed a passion for wood engraving – an archive of her woodcuts can be seen at Broughton House Gallery. Virginia Woolf described Gwen as 'All Cambridge, all Darwin, solidity, integrity, force and sense'. *(Cambridgeshire Collection, Cambridge Central Library)*

Girton College exterior. Girton was founded by Miss Emily Davies. Her first College for Women was initially established at Benslow House in Hitchin in 1869 and her hope was that Cambridge would eventually 'adopt the daughter'. Lecturers travelled by train to teach subjects such as Classics and Mathematics.

In 1871 another college for women established itself in rooms at 74 Regent Street near Parker's Piece, under the supervision of Miss Anne Clough. Miss Davies evidently thought this new development to be inferior and described its presence as a snake 'gnawing at our vitals'. Newnham College opened in 1875 on its present site, still under the direction of Miss Clough. Miss Davies had by then moved her school nearer to Cambridge. Girton opened its doors in 1873, on a site 2½ miles north-west of the city centre, as a fully residential Cambridge College for women. Before Girton none of the university colleges would admit women, which effectively prohibited them from studying for Cambridge degrees. In 1881 women were admitted to University exams but were still denied degrees or membership of the University proper.

Girton alumni include the novelist Rosamund Lehmann (1901–1990). After graduating she penned one of the most popular novels of the interwar years, *Dusty Answer*, which vividly depicts a young woman's experiences at Cambridge. Her later works *Invitation to the Waltz* (1932) and its sequel *The Weather in the Streets* (1936) were dramatised by the BBC in 1983. Some of her papers are held in the archives of King's College. The poet Kathleen Raine (1908–2003) was a Blare Research Fellow at Girton in 1926. *(Cambridgeshire Collection, Cambridge Central Library)*

The grounds of Girton College. *(Cambridgeshire Collection, Cambridge Central Library)*
    Possibly because of their 'out of town' location, female students were perceived as elusive:

. . . but where were they? The few that I clapped eyes on seemed capable of transferring themselves from the Sidgwick Avenue site to the safety of their Newnham sitting rooms within a matter of seconds, or else cycling back up Castle Hill to Girton as if competing successfully in the Tour de France.

Clive James, *May Week was in June*

Women students dining in hall. F.R. Leavis's wife Queenie Dorothy Roth (1906–81) was a research fellow at Girton working on *Fiction and the Reading Public*. She married the famous literary critic in 1929 and was arguably his primary motivating force. *(Cambridgeshire Collection, Cambridge Central Library)*

A view of Newnham College Gardens taken from Peile Hall looking towards the city centre, *c. 1920. (Cambridgeshire Collection, Cambridge Central Library)*

The experience of Cambridge for women is eloquently captured by Newnham graduate A.S. Byatt:

> There was the Cambridge of Ansell in *The Longest Journey*. And there was the Cambridge of *Dusty Answer*, a place of violent, suppressed, hopeless female passion and carefree golden young men. It is a town thick with words, wrapped in shining folds of words, alive with the history of words, and she never walked past the cows across the Cam from King's without hearing: 'The cow is there. She is there, the cow. Whether I'm in Cambridge or Iceland or dead the cow will be there. . . . It was philosophy. They were discussing the existence of objects.'
>
> A.S. Byatt, *The Virgin in the Garden*

New Hall, when based at Hermitage Hostel near Queens' College, *c. 1954. (Cambridgeshire Collection, Cambridge Central Library)*

In 1954 New Hall for women opened in Silver Street. Permanent buildings were established on the current site in 1962. The college claimed the first female University Vice-Chancellor, Rosemary Murray, in 1975.

The college was surely too distractingly pretty to be conducive to serious study.

P.D. James, *An Unsuitable Job for a Woman*

5

Grantchester Meadows

Students enjoying breakfast in The Orchard, Grantchester, probably photographed after
a May ball, 1950s. Grantchester is famously associated with Rupert Brooke but is within easy
walking distance of the colleges and is popular with students throughout the year.
(Cambridgeshire Collection, Cambridge Central Library)

Breakfast on the lawn in Grantchester – Brooke and friends. (*Reproduced by courtesy of the Rupert Brooke Society*)

Born on 3 August 1887 in Rugby, Rupert Chawner Brooke was the son of a schoolmaster. He came to King's College in 1906 with a scholarship to read Classics. Owing to its frequent appearance in his work, he is now more commonly associated with the pretty outlying village of Grantchester. The guest list at his home there reads like a literary or bohemian *Who's Who*.

'The Old Vicarage, Grantchester' reflects his sensitivity to the existence of previous poets in the idyll of remembered Grantchester:

> In Grantchester, in Grantchester . . .
> Still in the dawnlit waters cool
> His ghostly Lordship swims his pool,
> And tries the strokes, essays the tricks,
> Long learnt on Hellespont, or Styx,
> Dan Chaucer hears his river still
> Chatter beneath a phantom mill.
> Tennyson notes, with studious eye,
> How Cambridge waters hurry by . . .

The orchard in bloom. Rupert Brooke first came to Grantchester in 1909. Having completed his degree he moved out of his rooms in King's College into The Orchard, as a lodger of the Stevensons, who ran the Tea Garden. For 30s he was given two rooms, access to the gardens and all his meals. He spent an idyllic time in the village working at Shakespeare, reading, writing, wandering the woods and swimming every morning, and sometimes by moonlight, in the river. In 1909 he wrote to his friend Noel Oliver from The Orchard: 'at 10 p.m. (unless it's too horribly cold), alone, very alone and (though I boast of it next day) greatly frightened, I steal out, down an empty road, across emptier fields, through a wood packed with beings and again into the ominous open, and bathe by night. Have you ever done it?'

While his friends may have had mixed views on his poetry (Virginia Woolf terming it 'barrel-organ music'), Brooke was a charismatic, handsome and popular young man, and many friends sought him out in his rural retreat. They included E.M. Forster, Ludwig Wittgenstein, John Maynard Keynes, Augustus John, Virginia Woolf and Bertrand Russell. Keynes, visiting Brooke in November 1909, noted that he was sitting amid a host of admiring females wearing nothing but an embroidered sweater. (*Reproduced by courtesy of the Rupert Brooke Society*)

Byron's Pool, 1950s. *(Cambridgeshire Collection, Cambridge Central Library)*

In Brooke's well-known poem 'The Old Vicarage, Grantchester', 'His ghostly Lordship' is the poet Byron, who entered Trinity College, Cambridge, in 1805. Local legend tells that he was a frequent swimmer in the waters subsequently christened Byron's Pool and many people have retraced his journey to take a dip here.

The pool lies about half a mile upstream of the Old Vicarage near the boundary of Trumpington and Grantchester. It was one of Brooke's favourite places, where he, ever the romantic adventurer, often took his friends night-swimming.

In 1911 Brooke and Virginia Stephen (later to be Mrs Woolf) ventured to Byron's Pool and swam naked by moonlight. Virginia thought herself very daring. Brooke also took David Garnett, another Bloomsburyite and later Vanessa Bell's (Virginia's sister) lover, to swim there. Garnett later wrote about the experience: 'through the dew-soaked grass of the meadow over the mill-wall leading to the pool, to bathe naked in the unseen water, smelling of wild peppermint and mud'.

Opposite, top: A boating party – Bloomsbury on the Cam: Keynes, Woolf and Brooke, *c.* 1910. Virginia Woolf christened Brooke's friends the Neo-Pagans. Others later termed them the Grantchester Group, as so many were notable members of the so-called Bloomsbury Group. They were not always at ease with one another. In 1924 Woolf wrote of E.M. Forster, 'I always feel him shrinking from me, as a woman, a clever woman, an up-to-date woman.' *(Reproduced by courtesy of the Rupert Brooke Society)*

Opposite, bottom: The Orchard tea rooms. Planted in 1868, The Orchard became a tea garden when students on a day trip to Grantchester in 1897 asked the owner of the house, Mrs Stevenson, if she would serve them tea in her garden. She quickly realised the setting was ideal for a new business venture and The Orchard began to advertise as a popular visitor attraction. The tea pavilion is Edwardian. Students still punt up the river to Grantchester to have breakfast at The Orchard after the May Week Balls.

Tea drinkers here have included A.A. Milne, J.B. Priestley, Sylvia Plath, Ted Hughes, David Frost, Clive James, John Cleese and Salman Rushdie. *(Reproduced by courtesy of the Rupert Brooke Society)*

The Old Vicarage. Bought in 1853 by Samuel 'Page' Widnall, the Old Vicarage underwent a transformation. In 1857 Page constructed a folly, the 'Castle Ruin' (below), in the garden, which can be seen from the public footpath leading to the mill stream. Such a romantic rural retreat must have seemed near perfect to Brooke the young bohemian, and just before Christmas in 1910 he moved here to lodge with Mr and Mrs Neeve. At the time he wrote that 'the garden is a great glory', and that the house was 'an admirable ruin' despite its lack of drains. *(Cambridgeshire Collection, Cambridge Central Library)*

STANDS THE CHURCH CLOCK AT TEN TO THREE !

AND IS THERE HONEY STILL FOR TEA ?

Rupert Brooke.

ST ANDREW'S CHURCH, GRANTCHESTER.

The parish church of St Andrew and St Mary is a typically pretty English country church, and has strong links with Corpus Christi College. The monument to the fellows of the college interred in the churchyard carries a pelican, symbol of self-sacrifice, and part of the college coat of arms. Most of the church dates from the mid-fifteenth century. The clock was installed in about 1869, and draws many visitors, owing to Rupert Brooke's mention of it in his poetry.

One of many notable names buried here is a local woman, Anne Jemima Clough, who became the first Principal of Newnham College. She died in February 1891. *(Cambridgeshire Collection, Cambridge Central Library)*

Opposite, bottom: Widnall's folly, the 'Castle Ruin', at the end of the Old Vicarage garden. Brooke spent several years travelling and working at his poems and studies. His work was rewarded when on 8 March 1913 King's College made him a Fellow, the first non-Etonian Fellow in its history. It was a fertile time for Brooke. In May 1912 in the Café des Westens, Berlin, he composed one of his best-loved poems, 'The Old Vicarage, Grantchester'. It was first published in *Basileon*, the King's College magazine. Brooke himself termed it 'a masterpiece'.

Brooke's mother eventually bought the Old Vicarage and gave it to his friends Dudley and Annemarie Ward. They are buried in the church. *(Cambridgeshire Collection, Cambridge Central Library)*

Ah, God! To see the branches stir
Across the moon at Grantchester!
To smell the thrilling-sweet and rotten
Unforgettable, unforgotten,
River-smell, and hear the breeze
Sobbing in the little trees.
Say, do the elm-clumps greatly stand
Still guardians of that holy land?
The chestnuts shade, in reverend dream,
The yet unacademic stream?
Is dawn a secret shy and cold
Anadyomene, silver-gold?
And sunset still a golden sea
From Haslingfield to Madingley?
And after, ere the night is born,
Do hares come out about the corn?
Oh, is the water sweet and cool
Gentle and brown above the pool?
And laughs the immortal river still
Under the mill, under the mill?
Say, is there Beauty yet to find?
And Certainty? and Quiet kind?
Deep meadows yet, for to forget
The lies and truths, and pain?....... Oh! yet
Stands the church-clock at ten to three?
And is there honey still for tea?

                                        R. B.

Café des Westens. Berlin.   May. 1912.

The manuscript of 'The Old Vicarage, Grantchester'.

> Stands the church clock at ten to three?
> And is there honey still for tea?

In the first working of this poem Brooke wrote 'half past three'. Dr Mary Archer notes in her book *Rupert Brooke and The Old Vicarage, Grantchester* that he may have altered this to 'ten to three' because it is lighter in rhythm. Local legend also has it that the clock was not working during the time Brooke lived there and may have been set permanently at this time, though no record of this exists.

Lady Tansley, commenting in the *Cambridge News* in 1968, stated that in 1907 the clock had actually stopped at a quarter to eight and remained so until 1915, when Brooke died. As a tribute to him the clock was set at ten to three, where it stayed for many years. (*Rupert Brooke Trust and the Provost & Fellows of King's College, Cambridge*)

The 'phantom mill' of Brooke's poem 'The Old Vicarage, Grantchester'. *(Cambridgeshire Collection, Cambridge Central Library)*

It was near Byron's pool and is a reference to Chaucer:

At Trumpingtoun not fer fro Cantebrigge
Ther goth a brook and over that a brigge:
Upon the whiche brook ther stonne a mylle.

The nearby village of Trumpington and its mill appear in Chaucer's *The Reeve's Tale. (Cambridgeshire Collection, Cambridge Central Library)*

The story concerns the miller, his wife and daughter, and two Cambridge students. Sylvia Plath wrote to her mother saying she had recited all she knew of the tale to a field of Grantchester cows and Ted Hughes described in a poem how they appeared to be completely 'enthralled'!

The reference in Brooke's poem to Tennyson may have been in regard to his poem 'The Miller's Daughter', which also has a loose connection with Trumpington Mill:

The sleepy pool above the dam,
The pool beneath it never still . . .

Grantchester Meadows. The walk from Cambridge to Grantchester, traditionally known as the Grantchester Grind, has not deterred students seeking a diversion from their studies. Over the centuries some of our greatest literary figures have picnicked in its meadows and punted along and swum in its streams, including Tennyson, Wordsworth, Coleridge, Spenser, Marlowe, Milton, Byron, Virginia Woolf, Ted Hughes and Sylvia Plath. There is much evidence that Rupert Brooke and many others have both sensed and were inspired by the literary lure of Grantchester.

The village appears many times in Sylvia Plath's diaries and letters home to her mother in America in the 1950s. *(Cambridgeshire Collection, Cambridge Central Library)*

Opposite: The war memorial that bears Rupert Brooke's name. In September 1914, at the start of the First World War, Brooke signed up for active service in the Royal Naval Volunteer Reserve. On 28 February 1915 he sailed for Constantinople aboard the *Grantully Castle*. In March the ship docked at Port Said and it was here that Brooke first fell ill with dysentery. He also appears to have suffered a mosquito bite to the lip that led to blood poisoning. On 22 April he was put aboard a French hospital ship, the *Duguay-Trouin*, but died the next day, at the age of 27. He was buried in his uniform in an olive grove on the island of Skyros in the Aegean. *(S. Roberts Collection)*

The war memorial in Grantchester churchyard, built *c*. 1921, now shows the names of all those from the village who died in both world wars. Brooke is remembered on the memorial – 'men with splendid hearts' – and also on a plaque in Rugby School which carries the words of arguably his most famous poem, 'The Soldier':

> If I should die think only this of me,
> That there's some corner of a foreign field
> That is forever England.

In 1924 Bertrand Russell wrote sadly, 'It hurts reading of all that young world now swept away . . . in whom one thought at the time that there was hope for the world . . . Rupert himself loved life.' *(Cambridgeshire Collection, Cambridge Central Library)*

6

Postwar Poets, Novelists, Comics & Critics

Graduation Day. *(Cambridgeshire Collection, Cambridge Central Library)*

Clever was a Cambridge word . . . It had connotations of quick-wittedness and sharpness which the more neutral 'intelligent' lacked.

A.S. Byatt, *The Virgin in the Garden*

Gonville and Caius gateway. The sheer volume of literary talent passing through the gates of twentieth-century Cambridge is astounding. Playwrights include John Arden, Howard Brenton, Ronald Firbank, Simon Gray, Stephen Poliakoff, David Hare and Peter Shaffer. The university can lay claim to many significant poets too, such as William Empson, Elaine Feinstein, Gavin Ewart, Ted Hughes and J.H. Prynne. The list of authors is also long: Peter Ackroyd, Douglas Adams, J.G. Ballard, A.S. Byatt, Colin Dexter, Margaret Drabble, Sebastian Faulks, Nick Hornby, Christopher Isherwood, Michael Frayn, Howard Jacobson, Clive James, Rosamond Lehmann, A.A. Milne, Nicholas Monsarrat, Vladimir Nabokov, Sylvia Plath, Piers Paul Read, John Cowper Powys, J.B. Priestley, Salman Rushdie, Tom Sharpe, C.P. Snow, Graham Swift, Hugh Walpole and Patrick White. *(Cambridgeshire Collection, Cambridge Central Library)*

The Arts Theatre. Footlights launched in June 1883 with its first 'May Week Burlesque'. The very first Club Room was on Sidney Street; it then moved to Bridge Street, and from 1896 until the Second World War resided in Corn Exchange Street. An annual May Week show, a mixture of musical comedy and off-beat humour (in 1914 the review was entitled *Was It The Lobster?*), was held each year (except during the First World War) until 1935.

In 1936 the Arts Theatre (above) was completed and the Footlights settled into their new home. During the Second World War the company moved to the ADC near Sidney Sussex, returning to the Arts Theatre in 1948. *(Cambridgeshire Collection, Cambridge Central Library)*

The list of famous cast members is endless. Footlights has nurtured the writing, directing and performing talents of (to name just a few) Peter Cook, Jonathan Miller, John Cleese, Eric Idle, Emma Thompson, Stephen Fry, Hugh Laurie, Germaine Greer, Peter Hall, Clive James, Michael Frayn, Douglas Adams, John Bird, Ian McKellen, Michael Redgrave, Griff Rhys Jones, Sir Richard Eyre, Sir Peter Hall, Trevor Nunn, David Hare, Mike Newell, Howard Brenton (editor of the literary magazine *Look We Have Come Through* and controversial author of *Romans In Britain*). All cut their teeth on one Cambridge stage or another. *(Getty Images)*

The Footlights club-house was in Petty Cury, and played home to half of Monty Python – John Cleese, Graham Chapman and Eric Idle – in the 1960s. Clive James, author and broadcaster, was an active member and vividly recalls his introduction to the Society:

> The club held two smoking concerts (called smokers) each term. The first smoker of the first term was the chief audition smoker for new members. The club room was above MacFisheries fish shop in Falcon Yard, off Petty Cury. Required dress was a dinner jacket. . . .
>
> 'How do I join?' I asked. 'You don't,' he said though a barely controlled yawn. 'You audition.' Informing me that his name was Idle, he handed me a roneoed set of instructions saying where, when and how.'
>
> Clive James, *May Week was in June*

Clive James has written several volumes of memoirs that mention his time at Cambridge, including *Falling towards England* (1985) and *May Week was in June* (1990). *(Getty Images)*

Pembroke College. *(Cambridgeshire Collection, Cambridge Central Library)*

The Pembroke Players, a dramatic society founded in 1955, fostered the talent of some of the nation's best-loved comic writers. Peter Cook entered Pembroke College to read French and German in 1957. By 1960 he was President of the Cambridge University Footlights Club, creating sketches along with David Frost and John Fortune. The now famous Footlights revue, *Beyond the Fringe*, written and performed by Peter Cook, Dudley Moore, Alan Bennett and Jonathan Miller, opened at the Edinburgh Festival on 22 August 1960. The show transferred to the Fortune Theatre in London the following year and opened the way for the satirical comedy of the late twentieth century.

Clive James recalls the heady atmosphere in *May Week Was In June:*

> Of all the college smokers, the most reliably successful was the Pembroke smoker. When Peter Cook had been up, agents from London would attend the Pembroke smoker and try to purchase the material. On one occasion Cook sold the whole show to the West End. The effect of his professionalism, though not necessarily of his originality, had lingered on. It was a hard act to follow.

Sir David Hare (Jesus 1965) soaked up the dramatic atmosphere, attending talks by old boys Michael Frayn and Alfred Hitchcock. In 1975 he wrote *Teeth 'n' Smiles*. The play starred Helen Mirren and dealt with the division between the contemporary world and the archaic life of Oxbridge: 'For me, Cambridge was a waiting room before life began.' *(Getty Images)*

> David Hare, a brilliant talent with a capacity for organisation almost unheard of among undergraduates. . . . From the viewpoint of a politically committed young dramatist with big plans for a new British theatre of Brechtian social analysis, there was something irredeemably insignificant about Footlights.
>
> Clive James, *May Week was in June*

Footlights and the Cambridge stages have always attracted royal performers and writers, Prince Charles and Prince Edward both having appeared in revues during their student years here. Prince Charles was in residence at Trinity and Prince Edward at Jesus College. *(Cambridgeshire Collection, Cambridge Central Library)*

One thing she did not, in the end, do, was live in the Cambridge theatre world as she had dreamed of doing. This was one of the closed worlds, perpetually excited, with ambitious plans for the future and a gossip that reached out into the real world, or a part of it. They knew what they were doing and what they thought, their manner suggested openness and warmth, darling, they said, and love, in every other sentence.

A.S. Byatt, *The Virgin in the Garden*

Opposite: Stephen Fry (Queens' 1981), author, actor and playwright, was born in 1957. His novels often refer to his Cambridge years, including *The Liar* and *The Hippopotamus*. Fry came to Queens' College aged 20. It was at Cambridge that he met Hugh Laurie and Emma Thompson and in 1980/81 became a member of Footlights. They went on to perform their piece *The Cellar Tapes* at the Cambridge May Week Revue and the Edinburgh Festival Fringe, where they won the first Perrier Pick of the Fringe Award for Comedy. The company at that time also included Tony Slattery and Rowan Atkinson. Douglas Adams described the performance as having 'remarkably intelligent minds behind it' (*Guardian*, 1991). In the mid-1980s, Fry co-wrote the musical *Me and My Girl* and in 1998 starred in the film *Wilde* – a biopic of Oscar Wilde – which he described as 'the best professional thing I have ever done'. *(Hamilton Hodell Agency)*

Germaine Greer, in a portrait by Paula Rego (1995). The influential academic, writer and broadcaster, came up to Pembroke College in the 1960s to read for an English PhD. She was actively involved in student drama and a contemporary of Clive James at Pembroke and in Footlights. Her many works include *Kissing The Rod, The Female Eunuch* and, most recently, *The Boy*. She has lectured widely and held the post of Special College Lecturer in English at Newnham College, Cambridge.

Other influential modern Cambridge women include Elaine Feinstein. Described as fiercely internationalist in outlook, perhaps because of her Russian-Jewish origins, Feinstein's work extends to biography and translation – *Marina Tsvetayava* (1987) and an acclaimed novel, *Mother's Daughter* (1988), as well as volumes of poetry. *(National Portrait Gallery)*

Emma Thompson (Newnham, 1981), screenwriter, actor and Academy Award winner (best adapted screenplay, *Sense and Sensibility*, the film in which she also starred). She was a member of Footlights and appeared in a number of highly successful revues with her contemporaries, Hugh Laurie, Stephen Fry, Tony Slattery and Imelda Staunton. (*Hamilton Asper Agency*)

The poet Sylvia Plath was born on 27 October 1932 in America. Sadly, she is perhaps best known as wife to the late Poet Laureate, Ted Hughes, and for the manner of her death, by suicide, in 1963.

In 1950 she won a place at the Ivy League Smith College in Massachusetts. Her writing talents won her both a guest editorship of *Mademoiselle* in New York and, in 1955, a Fulbright Scholarship to Newnham College, Cambridge. She arrived in October with two intentions: to work, and to find an all-consuming love. She lived for a time in the Whitstead Hostel on Barton Road, shown here. *(Cambridgeshire Collection, Cambridge Central Library)*

Opposite, top: In February 1956 she met fellow poet Ted (Edward James) Hughes at the launch party for the *Saint Botolph's Review* (which Hughes founded with five friends). He was 25 and totally committed to his writing. They married in 1956 at St George the Martyr in Bloomsbury 'with nothing but love and hope in our own selves. . . . An empty church in the watery yellow-gray light of rainy London'.

They honeymooned in Paris, then returned to Cambridge and lived for a while in college rooms before moving to a flat in a house in Eltisley Avenue in Newnham village. Hughes found the academic regime at Cambridge uninspiring and it was after graduating that his poems began to appear in Cambridge magazines, including *Granta*, and to win important prizes, as with his first collection, *The Hawk in the Rain*. *(Peter Lofts, Ramsey and Muspratt)*

Opposite, bottom: 55 Eltisley Avenue, Newnham Village. By 1957 their association with Cambridge had ended. In December 1959 they set up home in Chalcot Square, Primrose Hill. In April 1960 Frieda Hughes was born and Sylvia's poetry collection, *The Colossus*, was sold to Heinemann. Sylvia was becoming increasingly frustrated with her life in London, and the family – they now also had a son, Nicholas – moved to Devon in 1961. In 1962 Plath and Hughes separated and Sylvia returned to London, setting up home in Fitzroy Square, Primrose Hill. She had writing commissions from the *New Yorker, Atlantic Monthly* and *Punch* but was becoming increasingly introspective. In February 1963, with reviews for *The Bell Jar* not wholly encouraging, Sylvia Plath killed herself. *(Cambridgeshire Collection, Cambridge Central Library)*

P.D. James was born in Oxford in 1920 and attended Cambridge High School for Girls. She has won awards for her crime writing all around the world, including Britain, Italy and America, where she was awarded the Mystery Writers of America Grandmaster's Award.

P.D. James was created a life peer in 1991, taking the title Baroness James of Holland Park. A selection of her many works is given at the end of this book. *An Unsuitable Job for a Woman* is set in Cambridge and describes the town with great beauty. *(Baroness James of Holland Park)*

A view of the Backs, looking towards Clare College and bridge. *(Cambridgeshire Collection, Cambridge Central Library)*

She was seeing Cambridge at its loveliest. The sky was an infinity of blue from whose pellucid depths the sun shone in unclouded but gentle radiance. The trees in the college gardens and the avenues leading to the Backs, as yet untouched by the heaviness of high summer, lifted their green tracery against stone and river and sky. Punts shot and curtsied under the bridges, scattering the gaudy water fowl, and by the rise of the new Garrett Hostel bridge the willows trailed their pale, laden boughs in the darker green of the Cam.

P.D. James, *An Unsuitable Job for a Woman*

A.S. Byatt, one of Britain's foremost writers. *(A.S. Byatt, Chatto & Windus and Michael Trevillion, The Trevillion Picture Library)*

Byatt's novel *Possession* won the Booker Prize in 1990 and has been adapted for the screen. She read English at Newnham College and was awarded a First. Having achieved the post of Senior Lecturer at University College London, she became a full-time writer in 1983 and was awarded a CBE in 1990 and DBE in 1999.

Byatt is often compared to Iris Murdoch (the writers knew one another and often debated the influence of Oxbridge upon their development). Her first critical work, *Degrees of Freedom*, was a study of Murdoch. On writing she says that she never wanted to do anything else: 'I grew up on *A Room of One's Own* and learned its practical lessons very hard.'

Her sister Margaret Drabble was born in 1939 and has written a number of widely acclaimed novels including *Seven Sisters* and *The Peppered Moth*. She also attended Newnham College and in 1980 she was awarded a CBE.

Byatt brings the Cambridge of her student years vividly to life:

Newnham was in those days outside, but nor far outside, Cambridge University proper. It had the proportions and atmosphere, with its Dutch red-brick gables, its corridors, landings, solid banisters and mansarded attics, of a comfortable country house. It had a civilised garden with roses, herbaceous borders, shrubbery, sunken pond. Frederica's room, austere and ladylike, looked out over this garden. Frederica was aware that the college was an agnostic foundation, which pleased her, though she was mainly ignorant of the struggles on behalf of women, the anxieties about Fellows in Holy Orders, the anguished battles of principle with God, the church and the university which had inspired Sidgwick and the other founders. Returning to Newnham in the 1970s Frederica saw it as beautiful – graceful in scale, civilised in space, humane.

A. S. Byatt, *The Virgin in the Garden*

Opposite: F.R. Leavis (1895–1978). *(Cambridgeshire Collection, Cambridge Central Library)*

Leavis was born at 68 Mill Road in Cambridge and went to the Perse School. His father ran a piano shop near the gates of Downing College. His influential *Mass Civilisation and Minority Culture* was published in 1930 and in 1932 Leavis was appointed Director of English Studies at Downing. There he published a periodical *Scrutiny* which he and his wife Queenie (née Roth, 1906–81) edited for twenty years. Always a controversial figure he became the best known and most acerbic literary critic of his time. (Leavis on Brooke: 'as vulgar as Keats with a public school accent'.) He was passionate about the ethical responsibility of great literature and this seriousness is evident in his studies of English, *The Great Tradition* (1948) and *The Common Pursuit* (1952). There is no doubt that Leavis made a considerable impact on Cambridge life. His radical approach made him a figure of admiration and abuse.

In life as in death . . . Leavis was the most contentious name in Cambridge.

A.S. Byatt

In favour of Dr Leavis, it has to be said that his Great Tradition of the English-language novel began with Jane Austen and had George Eliot – 'the English Tolstoy' – at its centre. I think this did more for my sense that women could be great writers without problems than all the subsequent feminist special pleading and corralling and inventing of 'women's writing'. In favour of Dr Leavis – and even more of I.A. Richards . . . the tradition of close reading, looking again and again at the meaning of words in their contexts – was a Cambridge invention. Good writers need to be good close readers.

A.S. Byatt

Leavis's views were almost impossible not to misrepresent, because they were designed so that only he could hold them.

Clive James

There's a strongly moralising strain to the Cambridge character, which came through in F.R. Leavis, whose influence was powerfully negative and virtually corrupted an entire generation of future critics, teachers and literary editors who read English . . .

J.G. Ballard

Dr Leavis was a bad influence on creative writing, in my view, and drove all the talent into the theatre in my Cambridge days. A good thing for the theatre though . . .

Margaret Drabble

There have been many other influential English lecturers and critics at Cambridge in the twentieth century.

Sir Arthur Quiller-Couch (1863–1944), shown above, was a Fellow of Jesus College in 1912 at the time of his election to the Chair of English Literature. Known as 'Q', he lectured in morning dress and had the disconcerting habit of addressing female students as 'gentlemen'. His influence on the development of Cambridge English can be extracted from his published letters, *On the Art of Writing* (1916) and *On the Art of Reading* (1920). He also edited the acclaimed *Oxford Book of English Verse* (1900). Quiller-Couch had rooms on C staircase, First Court. He was a founding father of the English Tripos in 1917. He was a friend of J.M. Barrie (1860–1937), a frequent visitor to Cambridge and best known as the author of *Peter Pan*.

Ivor Armstrong Richards (1893–1979) has been described as one of the 'leading Cambridge formative intellects of the twentieth century'. Richards was a poet, literary critic and founding father of the English Faculty of the University. He developed the now well-established technique of practical criticism (*Practical Criticism*, 1929). His methods are credited with encouraging the novel approach of reviewing poetry based purely on its own merits.

Raymond Williams (1921–88), Fellow of Jesus from 1961 and Professor of Drama, was a flamboyant Marxist, popular with students despite the fact that he often proved elusive to them!

C.S. Lewis (1898–1963) is probably best known for his fiction, such as *The Screwtape Letters* (1942) and works for children, such as *The Lion, The Witch and The Wardrobe* (1950). From 1954 he was Cambridge University Professor of Medieval and Renaissance Literature. He studied first at Oxford and adopted Cambridge and Magdalene College in his later years.

William Empson (1906–84) was Richards' pupil, studying under him at Magdalene. Having graduated in Maths at Cambridge Empson then transferred to study English. This may perhaps explain his incredibly detailed and analytical approach to the criticism of literature. His work *Seven Types of Ambiguity* (1929) was published to considerable acclaim and helped to win him a starred first. He was also a deft film and theatre reviewer and an accomplished poet. His work 'Sleeping Out in a College Cloister' was first published in the Magdalene College magazine. (*Getty Images*)

A department of the English Faculty. Cambridge English offers a diverse syllabus that allows the study of Arundhati Roy as well as Chaucer. It also includes important postwar figures such as Pinter, Rushdie and Seamus Heaney. I.A. Richards' concept, formulated in the 1920s, of starting with the 'words on the page' continues to influence Cambridge English. Richards started lecturing in the new school of English in 1919. His best-known work *Practical Criticism* (1929) used students' first-hand impressions of unattributed poems as its basis. Practical criticism is still considered to be the element of the Tripos that allows greatest insight into a student's 'literary sensibility'. Students study literature from 1300 to the present day and have freedom to research areas of interest in more detail. *(Author)*

BIBLIOGRAPHY & FURTHER READING

Cambridge Reference Texts

Archer, Mary, *Rupert Brooke and The Old Vicarage*, Grantchester, Silent Books, 1989

Chainey, Graham, *A Literary History of Cambridge*, Pevensey Press, 1985, 1995

Crosland, Margaret, *A Traveller's Guide to Literary Europe*, Hugh Evelyn, 1965

Drabble, Margaret, *A Writer's Britain: Landscape in Literature*, Thames & Hudson, 1979

Eagle, Dorothy and Cornell, Hilary (eds), *Oxford Illustrated Literary Guide to Great Britain and Ireland*, OUP, 1992

Hassall, Christopher, *Rupert Brooke – A Biography*, Faber & Faber, 1964

Keynes, Sir Geoffrey (ed.), *The Letters of Rupert Brooke*, Faber & Faber, 1968

Thomas, Edward, *A Literary Pilgrim in England*, 1917, rp OUP, 1980

Works and writers associated with Cambridge

Ackerley, J.R., *E.M. Forster: A Portrait*, Ranelagh Press, 1970

Ballard, J.G., *Empire of the Sun*, Gollancz, 1984

Bell, Quentin, *Virginia Woolf: A Biography*, Hogarth Press, 1972

Byatt, A.S., *The Virgin in the Garden*, Chatto & Windus, 1978

Chaucer, Geoffrey, *The Canterbury Tales*, Penguin, 1999

Dexter, Colin, *The Remorseful Day*, Macmillan, 1999

Conan Doyle, Sir Arthur, 'The Missing Three-Quarter', in *The Return of Sherlock Holmes*, George Newnes, 1905

Drabble, Margaret, *The Radiant Way*, Weidenfeld & Nicolson, 1987

Feinstein, Elaine, *The Ecstasy of Dr Miriam Garner*, Hutchinson, 1976

Fitzgerald, Edward, *Euphanor*, Pickering, 1851

Forster, E.M., *The Longest Journey*, Blackwood, 1907

——, *Howards End*, Edward Arnold, 1910

——, *Maurice*, Edward Arnold, 1971

Fry, Stephen, *Moab Is My Washpot*, Hutchinson, 1998

——, *The Liar*, Heinemann, 1991

Furbank, P.N., *E.M. Forster: A Life*, Secker & Warburg, 1977

Gray, Simon, *Simple People*, Faber & Faber, 1965

——, *Little Portia*, Faber & Faber, 1967

Hare, David, *Teeth 'n' Smiles*, Faber & Faber, 1976

Hewison, Robert, *Footlights! A Hundred Years of Cambridge Comedy*, Methuen, 1983

Howarth, L.S., *Ladies In Residence: A Novel of Cambridge*, Hodder & Stoughton, 1936

Hughes, Ted, *Birthday Letters*, Faber & Faber, 1998

Isherwood, Christopher, *The Memorial: Portrait of a Family*, Hogarth Press, 1932

——, *Lions and Shadows*, Hogarth Press, 1938

James, Clive, *Unreliable Memoirs*, Jonathan Cape, 1980

——, *Falling Towards England*, Jonathan Cape, 1985

——, *May Week was in June*, Jonathan Cape, 1990

James, P.D., *An Unsuitable Job for a Woman*, Faber & Faber, 1972

King, Francis, *E.M. Forster and his World*, Thames & Hudson, 1978

Kingsley, Charles, *Alton Locke*, Chapman & Hall, 1850

——, *Hereward the Wake*, Macmillan, 1866

Lee, Hermione, *Virginia Woolf*, Chatto & Windus, 1994

Lehmann, Rosamond, *Dusty Answer*, Henry Holt, 1927

Macaulay, Rose, *They Were Defeated*, Collins, 1932

Nabokov, Vladimir, *Glory*, Weidenfeld & Nicolson, 1972

Plath, Sylvia, *The Journals of Sylvia Plath 1950–1962*, Faber & Faber, 2000

——, *Letters Home*, Faber & Faber, 1975

Raphael, Frederic, *The Glittering Prizes*, Allen Lane, 1976

Raverat, Gwen, *Period Piece: A Cambridge Childhood*, Faber & Faber, 1952

St Aubyn, Alan, *Trollope's Dilemma: The Story of a Cambridge Quad*, 1889 (republished as *The Senior Tutor: A Story of a Cambridge Court*, F.V. White & Co, 1904.)

Sharpe, Tom, *Porterhouse Blue*, Secker & Warburg, 1974

Snow, C.P., *The Light and the Dark*, Faber & Faber, 1947

——, *The Masters*, Macmillan, 1951

——, *The Affair*, Macmillan, 1960

Stronach, Alice, *A Newnham Friendship*, Blackie & Son, 1901

Thackeray, W.M., *The History of Pendennis*, Bradbury & Evans, 1850

——, *The History of Henry Esmond*, Smith, Elder & Co., 1852

Trollope, Anthony, *John Caldigate*, Chapman & Hall, 1879

Unwin, F.T., *Cambridge Tales of Mystery and Mirth*, F.T. Unwin, 1983

Woolf, Virginia, *The Diary, vol. I 1915–19*, Hogarth Press, 1977

——, *Jacob's Room*, Hogarth Press, 1922

——, *The Letters*, vols I and II (ed. Nigel Nicolson), Hogarth Press, 1974/76

——, *A Room of One's Own*, Hogarth Press, 1929

——, *A Writer's Diary* (ed. Leonard Woolf), Hogarth Press, 1953

Wells, H.G., *The New Machiavelli*, Bodley Head, 1911

ACKNOWLEDGEMENTS

My grateful thanks to Dr Mary Archer, J.G. Ballard, A.S. Byatt, Colin Dexter, Margaret Drabble, Baroness James of Holland Park and Clive James, who were kind enough to send me their recollections of Cambridge and to allow me to quote from their works: P.D. James, *An Unsuitable Job for a Woman*, Faber & Faber, 2000 (1st pub. 1972); A.S. Byatt, *Still Life*, Vintage, 2003 (1st pub. 1985); Clive James, *May Week was in June*, Picador, 1990 (courtesy of Macmillan UK).

I would also like to thank the Rupert Brooke Society in Grantchester for their support. Gratitude is due to the staff of the Cambridge Central Library (Cambridgeshire Collection), particularly Chris Jakes, who made the research process so much easier.

My thanks as ever to Stuart and my family and to Simon Fletcher and Matthew Brown at Sutton Publishing for their editorial guidance, encouragement and, above all, patience.

Cambridge, Grantchester and Villages: Places to Visit

Rupert Brooke Museum and Orchard Tea Rooms, 45–7 Mill Way, Grantchester, Cambridge CB3 9ND, tel: 01223 551118.

Fitzwilliam Museum, Trumpington Street, Cambridge.

University and Colleges – collections and libraries usually by appointment only.

Cambridge Arts Theatre and The ADC – home of the Footlights Dramatic Society.